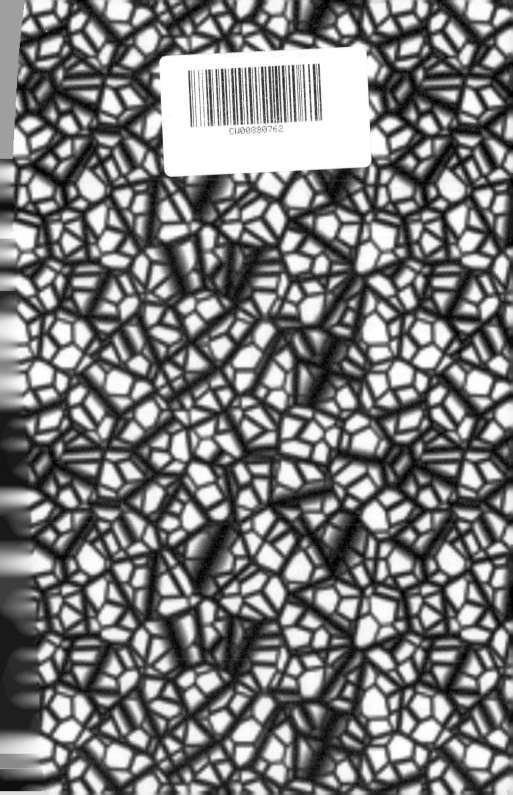

Front Cover Photography by **Kristaps B.**
www.flickr.com/photos/narciss/
Published by **.44 CALIBRE SHAKESPEARE**
http://**44calibreshakespeare.com**/

Three Tragedies by William Shakespeare
Copyright © 2010 Humphrey Bartosik

Inquiries should be addressed to .44 CALIBRE SHAKESPEARE;
Registered company in England & Wales: 7370506
info@44calibreshakespeare.com

This publication is one part of three from a complete title called
'Three Tragedies - by William Shakespeare'
ISBN of complete paperback publication: ISBN of this publication:
978-0-9567058-0-8   **978-0-9567058-5-3**

R&J Front cover : Kristraps B :
Beautiful 'Icywhite' girl : www.flickr.com/photos/narciss
R&J Prologue : Lo Scaligero :
Arch in the real Verona : http://it.wikipedia.org/wiki/Utente:Lo_Scaligero
R&J I.III : dbking :
Fireworks! : www.flickr.com/photos/bootbearwdc
R&J I.IV : Lo Scaligero :
Theatre of the real Verona : http://it.wikipedia.org/wiki/Utente:Lo_Scaligero
R&J II.I : Anne Burgess :
Garden wall stretching away : www.geograph.org.uk/profile/139
R&J II.III : Caesar Paes Barreto :
Roots : www.sxc.hu/profile/cesarpb
R&J II.V : Lo Scaligero :
Verona's Church : http://it.wikipedia.org/wiki/Utente:Lo_Scaligero
R&J III.II (mid) : Yusuf Ahmed :
Perfect legs : www.y-ahmed.blogspot.com
R&J III.II : Axel Rouvin :
Lightning strikes : www.flickr.com/photos/evdaimon
R&J III.V : Bryan Brenneman :
Two lovers : www.flickr.com/photos/434pics
R&J IV.I : Yusuf Ahmed :
Pale feet : www.y-ahmed.blogspot.com
R&J Commentary IV : Petr Kratochvil :
Rings : www.publicdomainpictures.net/browse-author.php?a=1
R&J V.III : Kristraps B :
Amazing 'Icywhite' girl again :www.flickr.com/photos/narciss
Rough Draft Font : Harold Lohner : www.haroldsfonts.com

. 44 CALIBRE SHAKESPEARE

presents

THE MOST EXCELLENT & LAMENTABLE TRAGEDY OF
ROMEO & JULIET

By William Shakespeare

Created by Humphrey Bartosik

DRAMATIS PERSONAE
REFERENCE PAGE
(IN ORDER OF APPEARANCE)

Sampson & Gregory, Capulet gang members

Balthasar & Abraham, Montague gang members

Benvolio, Montague's nephew and Romeo's homeboy

Tybalt, Lady Capulet's hot-headed nephew

Montague, Romeo's father, mafia boss

Lady Montague, Romeo's mother and Montague's wife

Capulet, Juliet's father, rival mafia boss.

Lady Capulet, Juliet's mother and Capulet's wife

Prince Escalus. He is the babylon in town

Paris, a young nobleman, rich sleezeball.

Romeo, teenage son of Montague

Mercutio, Romeo's crazy best friend

Juliet, Capulet's 13-year-old daughter

Nurse, Juliet's hysterical nanny

Friar Laurence, the local priest & herbologist

Peter, servant to Juliet's nurse

Apothecary, a pharmacist/drug dealer

The adventure continues at
http://44calibreshakespeare.com

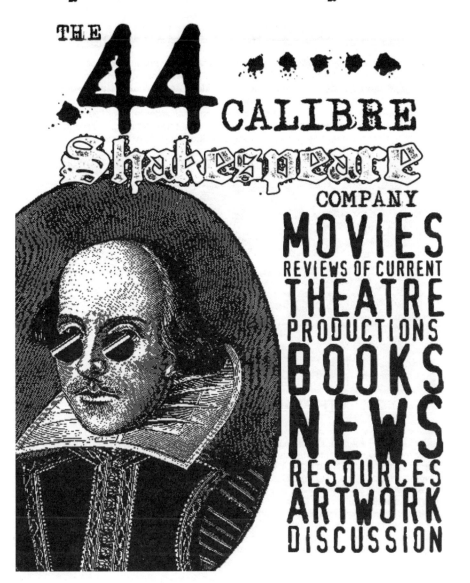

THE

.44

CALIBRE

Shakespeare

COMPANY

MOVIES

REVIEWS OF CURRENT

THEATRE

PRODUCTIONS

BOOKS

NEWS

RESOURCES

ARTWORK

DISCUSSION

GREAT ADVICE FOR ENJOYING SHAKESPEARE – IMPORTANT!

1. THE GOLDEN RULE : YOU KNOW BEST

The golden rule of Shakespeare is that no matter how I or anyone else interpret the plays nothing and I mean *nothing* should prevent you from having thousands of your own, *completely original,* downright marvellous ideas and thoughts that no-one else has ever thought of before. This is because in our own lives we all have our own individual *personal experiences* and it is those *personal experiences of yours* and no-one else's which are going to evoke & illuminate the true meaning, the wonder, the knowing, the might, the magic of Shakespeare within you.

2. LET THE LANGUAGE WASH OVER YOU

Shakespeare has a habit of using never ending sentences, that just go on and go on and on and on and on. First he starts saying something about this, then he quickly mentions this other thing, which is kind of amazing by itself and then he goes back to the original thing, completing the circuit and triggering an electrifying moment of realisation at the end of *the longest sentences known to man.* Gosh darn it, yes he does. Like the rain, the words and phrases and puns and references and double-meanings and antithesis are storming down on you and whether you like it or not you're going to get drenched, struck by lightning a few times and blown about by gale-force winds that nearly lift you off the ground – just give yourself over to the storm and take what you can from the experience. Even the most snobbish of scholars will only understand a *fraction* of any given play they have not studied themselves in depth, when seeing it performed live.

3. LISTEN TO THE BEAT (LIVE PERFORMANCES)

If watching Shakespeare, the trick of it requires precisely the same mental technique as that used to *actually listen to and comprehend lyrics* in music rather than just nod your head, humming along to a tune. It's really that simple. You just have to let go of this reality and flow with Shakespeare's. Do that, even for just a few seconds, and you will know what I'm talking about; all that noise in your head gets drowned out as your heart and mind tune in with what you are perceiving; the harmony is beautiful. One might say that the longer you can hold those moments for, the better you are doing. Typically, when people first get into Shakespeare they can only maintain this 'supra-concentration' I speak of for just a few seconds at a time, before having to relax for a few lines. After four years of recreational interest I can only manage about ten to fifteen minutes at a time before my consciousness drifts and when it drifts you will find it drifts in the direction of the profound things you are thinking about and how they relate to your own life. But what a rush, what a discovery, what an evolution those ten minutes are! Just like music, right?

4. ABOUT THE TEXT...

As you will see, on the left hand side of the page is the original Shakespearean script, transcribed and punctuated out of the quartos and folios, as all Shakespeare normally is. On the right hand side is the simplified explanation using modern language. I feel compelled to excuse the modern translation as no more than a clinical account of what the original script means, according to my own academic studies. Often, as best to capture the true essence of a meaning, I have included words that have no corresponding partner in the actual script. At other times I have used brackets to enclose information. Although I have had great fun searching for and trying to provide you with exactly the right choice of word(s) - to truly capture all the 'flavours' of any given phrase - I have also been forced to be quite repetitive, as sometimes middle-English has plenty of common words to describe something for which modern English has relatively few. No matter; the sterile trivialisation I have provided should be thought of as an intellectual key that can unlock the spiritual gateway of Shakespeare's mystic genius, which already lies dormant within you, long before you found this cool book.

Other 'translation' editions have been quite rightly criticised for 'replacing' the original Shakespeare, especially because they all grossly skim over the material and until now offer no actual annotations (as you will see in the brackets of this attempt). So it is that the reader ends up completely missing out on the Shakespeare and instead come to read and learn a horridly reduced, mutated clone that does not even make them use their brains in the special ways we will be exploring. I have used many methods to try and prevent this from happening, as I am painfully aware of the danger; the character names must be read with the original script therefore assuring constant involvement, the original script is on the left hand side of the page i.e. where we always begin reading a page from, brackets are always filled with italics to make the locating of annotations easy and not a matter of trawling through the entire stanza, the translation is deliberately clinical and scientific where the original is fun and imaginative, and wherever possible (due to the absolutely plain, simple and apparent meaning of the original text) I have omitted any translation at all, thus forcing the reader to trace the original and diverge into the translation whenever necessary.

However, the better for you to enjoy it, please make no mistake ; – the translation provided is, and always was intended to be, the very best and most accurate textual-supplement that has ever been attributed to Shakespeare. It seeks to be the clearest, the most explicit, *the definitive companion,* a key for anyone to use. If this is not the case, please believe me as I hope to be saved I will rejoice to know of the helping hand we have been deprived of thus far, by those scholars apparently seeking to keep Shakespeare all to themselves.

♦

Shakespeare In Da Hood

During the course of my studies, for what exact reason I'm not sure, I kept a log of the slang I came across which I know is still used in modern day London today. There is a lot to be said for the use of 'ghetto speak' in trying to understand the mentality with which Shakespeare was crafting his words. For instance, Jamaicans speaking Broken English, to which our newly-emerging 21st century street dialects owe the most inspiration by far in America as well as England, will have a very good natural understanding of the manner in which Shakespeare twists and turns, reverses and breaks-up words, using them out of context but in ways which are unmistakeably apt. I can confidently affirm that in spoken conversation Jamaicans enjoy an especially elastic use of the English language, individuals coining endless phrases and adjectives on a daily basis.

Remember; at the time Shakespeare wrote his plays the English language was still very much in the womb. English was the language of the peasants, barely spoken by the upper classes who would speak amongst themselves in French if royalty or Latin if holy. Shakespeare, writing for his punters, for the lower-classes, he drew on everything from Norwegian to German, Italian to French, Latin to Celtic and he amalgamated them all in the style he wrote in, constantly making up words which 'needed no explanation', basically creating the English language as we know it today. His style of language evokes the meaning phonetically. This is where many actors fall down in their pursuit of cracking the Shakespeare code because they think it is a matter of definition, like most language-based art is. But in fact, I propose, that the African, Arabic, Caribbean and even Orient mentalities, equipped as they are with 'looser' more 'fluid', 'hectic', 'mystifying', 'ambiguous', 'emotive' languages, are in fact closer to the natural approach required in attempting to truly grasp the magic in Shakespeare's choice of words.

Nowhere is this more evident than in rap music, which clearly has strong Caribbean and African roots ['toastin' as it was once called] and which is no less than the very same recipe which Shakespeare was cooking; selecting really interesting words, particularly currently fashionable contemporary ones, using the smallest amount of words possible to communicate the most complex meaning achievable whilst still being clear, making sure a good dollop of fiery emotion is mixed into the broth, all to conjure up a feeling, an emotion within the hearer by using no more than words to take them there and giving the whole thing a rhythm, a heart-beat, 'Iambic Pentameter' in Shakespeare's case, 'flow' in the rappers.

Our current lifestyle of total instant comprehension –on computers, on television, in adverts, in magazines and newspapers with text messages and e-mails and search engines– what I call 'the fibre-optic mentality' has resulted in an unnecessary 'fear' of Shakespeare. This needn't be so because the scripts were jolly well intended to be baffling. As long as one opens their ears to listen pretty much anybody is capable of seeing the magic. I am suggesting that because we do not understand every word of Shakespeare then we decide not to understand at all, rejecting the entire script because we can only understand half or less than half of it, in precisely the same way a posh white man might have difficulty appreciating rap music because he rejects the confusion of not understanding half or less than half of everything being said – what I am also suggesting, is that that little half or less than half which you might just grasp is so precious and powerful and inspiring that it's worth sitting through all the other jibberish anyway!

The following extracts are examples of where a youth from South London would actually have a superior understanding of the text than a professor from a university who was not aware of the use of that word in context today and certainly never used it themselves, whereas the ghetto youth might use it on a daily basis and therefore attribute far greater relevance to the use of that particular word. When I use the term 'common hood phrase' I mean a term used in those places of our country that qualify as 'the street' to a significant number of people, used every day and probably something you shouldn't write in an English essay for your teacher. Hehehe this should be fun. More coming soon.

Iago (Othello): *Say no more.* / 'Say no more' is a common hood phrase, often used to cut short a tiresome or possibly incriminating conversation. **Desdemona (Othello):** *If I court moe women, you'll couch with moe men!* /'Mo hydro', 'Mo fyah', 'mo' meaning 'more'. **Othello:** *Let it alone* / 'Let it alone' meaning 'forget about it' is a common yardy phrase. **Desdemona (Othello):** *This Lodovico is a proper man.* **Orlando (As You Like It):** *...to speak more properly.* **Phebe (As You Like It):** He'll make a proper man/ 'Proper' meaning 'very good' particularly used where the correct English would normally be 'properly', '*He done that job proper*', '*His bars are proper bruv,*' **Gratiano (Othello):** *Some good man bear him carefully from hence.* **Diana (All's Well):** *By Jove, if ever I knew man, 'twas you* /'Man' meaning 'men in general' is commonly used in the hood; '*Man is out ere*', '*Some man are on dis fing*'. **Cassio (Othello):** *...and squabble? swagger? Swear?* **Puck (A Midsummer Night's Dream):** *What hempen home-spuns have we swaggering here?* /'Swagger' meaning 'highly apparent self-confidence' is a common hood phrase. **Iago (Othello):** *Nay, you must forget that* / 'Forget that' is commonly used in the hood to dismiss an idea or notion. **Othello:** *Honey, you shall be well desired in Cyprus* / 'Honey' is notorious slang for 'darling', 'baby', for instance, in music by Alexander O'Neal. **Othello:** *Holla! Stand there!* / 'Holla' is notorious hood slang for attracting someone's attention, usually an attractive woman's; *'Holla back!'* **Hamlet:** *...it hath made me mad.* Dromio of Ephesus [Comedy of Errors]: *It would make a man mad as a buck* / 'Mad' meaning 'angry' or 'extremely', 'very', is commonly used in the hood **Claudius [Hamlet]:** *Oh this is the poison of deep grief.* The Rape of Lucrece: *Deep woes roll forward like a gentle flood* /'Deep meaning 'serious' or 'extremely harsh'; *'That is deep blud'*, *'that was mad deep of her '*. Titus Andronicus: *Welcome, dread Fury, to my woeful house.* Hamlet: *The important acting of your dread command?* / 'Dread' meaning 'seriously bad' or 'deadly serious'; *'that is dread '*, *'when she slapped him it was maa-a-ad dread '* **Hamlet:** *...the cat will mew and dog will have it's day* / 'every dog has it's day' is a common hood phrase, often expressed about someone who has achieved short-lived financial success through undesirable means **Romeo:** *...that fall back to gaze on him/* 'Fall back' meaning 'retreat' or 'move away from', *you should fall back blud'* **Romeo:** *I'll tell thee, ere thou ask it me again.* /'ask it me' is obviously poor English [it should be 'ask it of me'] but a typical example of a phonetically more powerful simplification of a term; *'you never ask it me or I would have done it '*, *'Ask it me again and I'll give you a slap '* **Romeo:** *tempt not a desperate man* / 'tempt not a desperate man' is a common hood phrase. Nurse [R&J]: *Where's my man?* Tybalt [R&J]: *Here comes my man* / 'My man' is a very common hood phrase, for instance, it was used by Denzel Washington in *American Gangster* 2007. **Henry V:** *a box 'o th' ear!* / *'I boxed him in his ear '*, 'box' meaning 'struck' is a common hood phrase. **Ariel (The Tempest):** *Say what; what shall I do?* / 'Say what' meaning 'explain that please' is a common hood phrase **Luciana [Comedy of Errors]:** *Fie, beat it hence!* / 'Beat it' meaning 'go away' is a common hood phrase, for instance, Michael Jackson's song from the album 'Thriller, 1982'. **Iachimo [Cymbeline]:** *Believe it, sir, I have seen him in England* / 'Believe it' is a common hood phrase used to intensify meaning, *'You better believe it '* **Lucio [Measure for Measure]:** *You are too cold.* First Lord [Cymbeline]: *Your lordship is the most patient man in loss, the most coldest that ever turned up ace.* **Duke Solinus [Comedy of Errors]:** *If he were mad, he would not plead so coldly* / 'Cold' being used as an adjective for 'emotionally indifferent', 'serious' or 'to be cold hearted' is one of the most common of all hood phrases, *'How could you be so cold?'*, *'That girl's tattoo was cold '*, *'His bars are cold '*. **Katherina (The Taming of the Shrew):** *Comb your noodle* / 'Noodle' meaning 'head' is a phrase used by even the most gangster. **Queen Elizabeth [Richard III]:** *Harp on it still shall I till heart-strings break.* Hastings [Richard III]: *...yet think not on it.* Lucio [Measure for Measure]: *He arrests him on it* / 'On it' meaning 'going about it' or 'willing to do it', particularly in a mischievous, daring sense, *'Was she on it then?'*. **Rosalind [As you like it]:** *Love hath made thee a tame snake.* Holofernes [Loves Labours Lost] : *...his enter and exit shall be strangling a snake* /Although 'snake' is obviously a term for 'deceiver' in most languages, it is still a favourite term in the hood today and is used frequently. **Iago:** *And, I'll warrant her, fun of game.* Romeo:*The game was ne'er so fair and I am done/* 'Game' meaning 'feminine sexuality'. **Parolles [All's Well]:** *This is hard and undeserved measure, my lord.* Boyet [Love's Labour Lost]: *You are too hard for me.* 'Hard' meaning 'tough' and specifically 'unusual'. **Romeo:** *let me have A dram of poison, such soon-speeding gear/* 'Gear' referring to drugs, particularly illegal ones. **Iago:** *He hath a person and a smooth dispose To be suspected/* 'Smooth' meaning 'charming', 'sexually attractive', 'cool'. **Sailor:** *What, ho!* Iago: *Some wine, ho!* Cassio: *Oh help, ho!* Mercutio: *Come, we burn daylight, ho!* Friar John: *Brother, ho!/* 'Ho!' is the equivalent of 'yo!' and is used as regularly as it's street-counterpart is today. **Iago:** *She'll find a white that shall her blackness hit/* 'To hit' on somebody is to make an obviously flirtatious remark to somebody you wish to sleep with. **Prince Henry [Henry IV Part 1]:** *Pray God you have not murdered some of them.* Falstaff: *Nay, that's past praying for: I have peppered two of them;* / 'Peppered' meaning 'brutally injured' is hard in the hood. **Falstaff: I have led my ragamuffins** / 'Ragamuffin' is very hood. **Hamlet:** *Bring with thee airs from heaven or blasts from hell* / 'Blast' to 'shoot'. **Iago:** *for, 'Certes,' says he...*/'Certe', although used as Latin by Shakespeare is spelt and pronounced the same as an abbreviation for 'certified', especially in relation a person's worthiness proven; 'Can he be trusted?' '-Don't worry, he's certe.' **'Score'** as a word for the unit 20 is rarely used by the gentry of today but is probably more common in the hood than is the use of the actual word for that number and **'till'** as an abbreviation of 'until' is no less dominant. One more thing; hoodies were not invented in the 70's by Kool Herc or Run DMC ; there is *nothing* more English than the Medieval monk, sister, soldier, bandit, aristocrat, peasant, magus, witch or rider donning their cloak and hood as they step out into a bloody world of anarchy and Holy law for another day of ruthless survival. Even our Bishops and Kings wore them once.

♦

Two households, both alike in dignity,
In fair Verona, where we lay our scene,
From ancient grudge break to new mutiny,
Where civil blood makes civil hands unclean.
From forth the fatal loins of these two foes
A pair of star-cross'd lovers take their life;
Whose misadventured piteous overthrows
Do with their death bury their parents' strife.
The fearful passage of their death-mark'd love,
And the continuance of their parents' rage,
Which, but their children's end, nought could remove
Is now the two hours' traffic of our stage;
The which if you with patient ears attend,
What here shall miss, our toil shall strive to mend.

Romeo & Juliet

The tale of Juliet and her Romeo is more than just a play, it is the very essence and spirit of young, forbidden love. Can you remember the first time someone broke your heart? No matter how devastating it might have been, don't you still hold those memories precious and dear and vital? Doesn't that naïve, hasty, romantic fool you once were seem so excellent to the cynical old grump you are now? I'll tell you who Romeo & Juliet are: they are the last days of honest romance in a young man's life, the first days of true love in a girl's. I mean the kind of love where you sit there staring at each other for hours and hours on end, the kind of love where you feel stirring compassion for the world, the kind you honestly believe is special and unique to you. The kind that you know no-one else will ever quite believe how special it was. You know, the *first* love.

"My only love sprung from my only hate
Too early seen unknown and known too late."

Now make no mistake, despite it all ending in tears, *Romeo & Juliet* is most certifiably and irrefutably a romantic comedy. Look at the bozos at the start! Look at the babbling Nurse and the enlightened Friar! The hopelessly Italian mafioso families and the hilarious, ridiculous, absurd, wonderful and downright diabolically marvellous Mercutio! It should be noted that *true seriousness* lies in *humour*. In real life, we all make jokes the whole time. Even in the most violent, disturbing, triple academy award winning four hour war epic it's those little amusing moments between characters that really build a relationship with the audience. If every single line is snarled with a mean 1940's film noir accent, special FX popping out of people's ears and not a single realistic or even interesting character with anything to say, you sit there watching this stuff for two and a half hours then can't even remember ten minutes of it the next day. It's garbage for the brain, it's popcorn, bubblegum, it's not what you need to be eating if you intend to get up early the next morning for your run along the river before your appointments, followed by a late night flight to Monaco, where you're joining your business partners at a Grand Prix tournament to close a deal that's going to pay for your grand-children's inheritance –you get me? Shakespeare is. Anyway, in *Romeo & Juliet* Shakespeare exploits this empathy we feel for characters who can make us laugh by building up extravagant hysterias of jokes and knavery, splicing the language with endlessly long, sweeping romantic sentences. Once we see it in this light - as a romantic comedy - it allows the experience to become generally more entertaining. It should make us laugh - it's damn funny.

But despite the clear intentions at humour that dominate most of the play, there stand among those cheerful lines haunting allusions like hooded old boney standing still in a carnival of colourful motion, unseen by the merry participants all around him, nodding knowingly at us, his marble fingers outstretched, pointing the way to a shared grave. Among many other things, *Romeo & Juliet* is also a matter of destiny, of the guiding forces, of the strumpet fortune that leads some to the highest peak of Everest and others to the lowest cavern of Hades. Shakespeare juggles the audience's emotions like flaming swords, hopping from one hand to the other, everybody's intentions shooting around and colliding with each other amid a fierce melee of rapier wit and desperate measures.

"I defy you, stars!"

Romeo & Juliet offers us a chance to revisit that desperate first love. It dissects the anatomy of the mind in the meticulous way only Shakespeare can, each sentence striving forward in an unstoppable montage of humanity's inner-workings. In this play we hold the little life of young romance in the palm of our hand for just one moment, before it darts away again like a butterfly in the sunshine. Reading and understanding the passages is treasure for anyone who dares to claim it and as you embark on this journey be aware that like Merlin and Arthur, Shakespeare is always uttering his incantations over us, teaching us how to tear the sword from the stone and wield the true power of humanity that lies within.

ACT I

<table>
<tr>
<td valign="top">

Verona's Streets.
Enter Sampson & Gregory,
of the House of Capulet,
armed with swords.

Sampson
Gregory, o' my word, we'll not carry coals.

Gregory
No, for then we should be colliers.

Sampson
I mean, an we be in choler, we'll draw.
Gregory
Ay, while you live, draw your neck out o' the collar.
Sampson
I strike quickly, being moved.
Gregory
But thou art not quickly moved to strike.
Sampson
A dog of the House of Montague moves me.
Gregory
To move is to stir; and to be valiant is to stand:
therefore, if thou art moved, thou runn'st away.
Sampson
A dog of that house shall move me to stand: I
will take the wall of any man or maid of Montague's.

Gregory
That shows thee a weak slave;
for the weakest goes to the wall.

Sampson
True; and therefore women, being the weaker
vessels are ever thrust to the wall: therefore I will
push Montague's men from the wall and thrust his
maids to the wall.

Gregory
The quarrel is between our masters and us their men.

</td>
<td valign="top">

*The scene is **out in the street**,*
    *in the small Italian town of **Verona***
(which is a real place in Northern Italy).
    Enter a couple of jokers with some swagger,
representing for the Capulet family, armed up.

Gregory, I swear down, nobody's gonna make us
(*carry coals : sweat like we're heaving bags of*
coal around, 'suffer indignity' the phrase means
you are not in the mood to be abused by anyone).

Na (*we won't put up with anyone's nonsense*),
'cuz then we would be getting our hands dirty (*in*
the sense coal is grimy / to get your 'hands
dirty' means you would have to do something
undesirable i.e. not retaliate and be made to look
foolish by someone abusing them) .

What I'm saying is, if we get into a hype
(*confrontation*), I'm ready to pop off (*engage*).

That's it, just as long as you stay away from the
hangman's noose.

I hit 'em up (*attack*) real quick (*without*
hesitation), when I feel to.

But you're not real quick to feel to.

Any of that Montague lot and I'll be moved
(*provoked*) [to fight them].

To move is to run and to be tough is stand: so, if
you're 'moved' you're running away.

A dog from that crew would move me to stand; I
will (*take the wall : the streets of old cities were*
notoriously filthy and so those hanging out on the
street would stand close to the walls, where the
path was cleaner. Sampson is saying he will take
a Montague's place and push them out into the
muddy street, a common way of insulting
someone) of any man or woman of Montague's.

That's weak! (*'for the weakest...' : Old English*
Proverb, derived from the Coventry Mystery
Plays: "...the weykist gothe eyuer to the walle..."
The term means 'the weak will be overcome by
the strong' like 'survival of the fittest', probably
referring to Church services where the powerful
would sit at the front in pews and the poor would
be pushed back to the rear of the building).

True stories – that's why women, being (*weaker*
*vessels : **1 Peter 3:7**) weaker than men, are often
thrust to the floor (*such as in kinky sex*): so in
that case I will throw Montague's men away from
the wall (*as they are already the weakest*) and
grind his women against the wall (*a good reason*
for going to the wall, despite it being degrading).

The fight is between our bosses and us, their
men (*not their women*).

</td>
</tr>
</table>

Sampson
'Tis all one, I will show myself a tyrant:
    when I have fought with the men,
I will be cruel with the maids and cut off their heads.
Gregory
    The heads of maids?
Sampson
    Ay, the heads of maids, or their maidenheads;
take it in what sense thou wilt.
Gregory
    They must take it in the sense that feel it.
Sampson
    Me they shall feel while I am able to stand:
and 'tis known I am a pretty piece of flesh.
Gregory
    'Tis well thou art not fish; if thou hadst,
    thou hadst been Poor John. Draw thy tool!
    Here comes two of the house of Montagues!
Sampson
    My naked weapon is out: quarrel, I will back thee.
Gregory
    How? turn thy back and run?
Sampson
    Fear me not.
Gregory
    No, marry; I fear thee!
Sampson
    Let us take the law of our sides; let them begin.
Gregory
    I will frown as I pass by and let them take it as
                            they list.
Sampson
    Nay, as they dare. I will bite my thumb at them;
which is a disgrace to them, if they bear it.

            Enter Abraham & Balthasar
Abraham
    Do you bit your thumb at us, sir?
Sampson
    I do bite my thumb, sir.
Abraham
    Do you bite your thumb at us, sir?
Sampson [aside to Gregory]
    Is the law of our side, if I say ay?
Gregory
    No.
Sampson
    No, sir, I do not bite my thumb at you sir,
                but I bite my thumb sir.
Gregory
    Do you quarrel, sir?

It doesn't make a difference, I'll show you I'm a real monster: after I've fought [and killed] their men, I will be cruel with their maids and cut off their heads.

Cut off their maid's heads??!!

Yeah, cut off the heads of maids or their [*maidenheads : virginity*], take it however you want to.

They're gonna have to take it however you give it [*deliberate sexual slur*].

They'll feel me as long as I am able to stand [*keep my erection*]: everyone knows I'm hung [*pretty piece of flesh : well-endowed*].

It's good you're not a fish, 'cuz if you were you'd be a salty dried up bit of hake - Get your arms out! Here come two of d'em Montague boys!

My [*naked : unsheathed*] weapon is ready: do your thing, I've got your back.

How? By turning your back and running away?

Don't worry about me.

No, I'm serious, I worry about you.

Let's make sure the law takes our side [*if police get involved*]; let them make the first move.

I'll screw when they come past and they can take it however they want.

Na, however they dare. I will bite my thumb at them, which is a liberty if they take it.

*Enter two men from the House of Montague.
Sampson bites his thumb at them straight away.*

Are you biting your thumb at us, boss?

I am biting my thumb, *boss*.

Are you biting your thumb at us, *boss*?

Is the law on our side if I say yes?

No.

No, boss, I do not bite my thumb at you boss, but I bite my thumb, boss.

Are you starting a fight, boss?

3

Abraham

   Quarrel sir! No, sir.

A fight sir?! No sir.

Gregory

   If you do, sir, I am for you:

      I serve as a good a man as you.

'Cuz if you are, sir, I'm coming for you. I work for as fine as man as you do.

Abraham

   No better.

No better.

Sampson

   Well, sir.

[*Sampson runs out of steam*]

Gregory *[aside to Sampson]*

   Say 'better':

      here comes one of my master's kinsmen.

Say 'better',
  here comes one of our bosses' main men.

Sampson

   Yes, better, sir.

Yes, better, *boss*.

Abraham

   You lie.

Lies.

Sampson

   Draw, if you be men.

   Gregory, remember thy swashing blow.

C'mon, let's have it, if you're man enough. Gregory, remember to go hard.

      They fight bravely.

      Enter Benvolio

They brawl. Benvolio, a top dog in the Capulet gang, comes across them at it...

Benvolio

   Part, fools! Put up your swords,

      you know not what you do.

Break it up, you idiots! Put away your swords, you don't know what you're doing.

      Benvolio beats down their swords.

      Enter Tybalt

Benvolio beats down their swords and breaks it up. That's when the real trouble starts...

Tybalt

  What, art thou drawn among these heartless hinds?

Turn thee, Benvolio, look upon thy death.

What, you've pulled your blade on these cowardly dogs? Turn around, Benvolio, and look upon your death.

Benvolio

   I do but keep the peace: put up thy sword,

Or manage it to part these men with me.

I'm just keeping the peace; put away your sword or use it to help me break this lot up.

Tybalt

  What, drawn and talk of peace! I hate the word,

As I hate hell, all Montagues, and thee:

      Have at thee coward!

Eh? Draw my sword and then talk about 'peace'? I hate the word, like I hate hell, all Montagues and you: Have at it coward!

      They fight.

  Enter many of both houses who join the fray;

  then enter Citizens, crying 'Clubs! Clubs!'

Brawling on the street, more gang members arrive, some citizens get involved trying to put a stop to it and while this chaos erupts, old Capulet and his wife appear on the scene...

First Citizen

   Clubs, bills and partisans! strike! beat them

down! Down with the Capulets!

      Down with the Montagues!

[*'Clubs!'* : *'Stop fighting!'* , a phrase used by civilians to break up combatants]

      Enter Capulet & Lady Capulet

Capulet

   What noise is this? Give me my long sword, ho!

What's going on here? Get me my sword, yo!

Lady Capulet
> A crutch, a crutch! Why call you for a sword?

Capulet
> My sword, I say! Old Montague is come
> And flourishes his blade in spite of me.

Get him a crutch – what do you need a sword for [*she does not want her husband to fight*]?

My sword, I say! Old Montague has come and is waving his sword around, to insult me.

> Enter Montague & Lady Montague

Montague
> Thou villain Capulet – Hold me not, let me go.

Lady Montague
> Thou shalt not stir a foot to seek a foe.

You villain Capulet! Don't hold me, let me go!

You will not [*are not allowed to*] stir a foot to seek a foe [*'make any kind of deliberate effort to provoke an enemy'*].

> Enter Prince w Royal Guard

> Enter the Prince [*who is the law in town*]
> with his personal troop of soldiers
> [*by now there is full scale riot going on*].

Prince
> Rebellious subjects, enemies to peace,
> Profaners of this neighbour-stained steel – will they
> not hear? What, ho! you men, you beasts, that quench
> the fire of your pernicious rage with purple fountains
> issuing from your veins on pain of torture, from those
> bloody hands throw your mistemper'd weapons to the
> ground and hear the sentence of your moved prince.
> Three civil brawls, bred of an airy word, by thee, old
> Capulet, and Montague, have thrice disturb'd the
> quiet of our streets: If ever you disturb our streets
> again, your lives shall pay the forfeit of the peace. For
> this time, all the rest depart away: You Capulet; shall
> go along with me: And, Montague, come you this
> afternoon to know our further pleasure in this case.
> Once more, on pain of death, all men depart.

Rebels, enemies of peace, unworthy users of bloodied steel [*swords*] – won't they listen?! Oi! You men, you beasts that are so thirsty for blood that you spill purple fountains of blood from your veins, on pain of torture throw your [*mistempered : angry*] weapons to the ground and hear the judgement of your prince! Three times we've had open fighting in the street, all because of the warmongering between you, Old Capulet and Montague and three times has this disturbed our quiet neighbourhoods: if ever this happens again you will die in order to keep the peace. For now, everyone leave! You, Capulet, will come with me and you, Montague, come this afternoon and I'll tell you what else I've decided. Last warning, stay and die, every man leave now.

> Exeunt all save Montague,
> Lady Montague and Benvolio

Montague
> Who set this ancient quarrel new abroach?
> Speak, nephew, were you by when it began?

Benvolio
> Here were the servants of your adversary, and
> yours, close fighting ere I did approach: I drew to part
> them: in the instant came
> The fiery Tybalt, with his sword prepared,
> Which, as he breathed defiance to my ears,
> He swung about his head and cut the winds,
> Who nothing hurt withal hiss'd him in scorn:
> While we were interchanging thrusts and blows,
> Came more and more and fought on part and part,
> Till the prince came, who parted either part.

Who set off this old grudge again [*abroach : opening a bottle of liquor or gunpowder*]? Talk, nephew, were you here when it started?

There were the servants of your enemy and your own servants fighting when I got here – I came to break it up but a second later the hot-headed Tybalt, with his sword already drawn, and baiting me, swung around his head but only managed to cut the winds, which hurting nobody meant they hissed at him in scorn. While we were fighting, more and more people came and joined different sides until the Prince came who split both sides apart.

Lady Montague
> O, where is Romeo? saw you him to-day?
> Right glad I am he was not at this fray.

Where is Romeo? Have you seen him today? I'm glad he wasn't mixed up in this fight.

Benvolio

  Madam, an hour before the worshipp'd sun
Peer'd forth the golden window of the east,
A troubled mind drave me to walk abroad;
Where - underneath the grove of sycamore
That westward rooteth from the city's side -
So early walking did I see your son:
Towards him I made, but he was ware of me
And stole into the covert of the wood:
I, measuring his affections by my own,
That most are busied when they're most alone,
Pursued my humour not pursuing his,
And gladly shunn'd who gladly fled from me.

Montague

  Many a morning hath he there been seen,
With tears augmenting the fresh morning dew,
Adding to clouds more clouds with his deep sighs;
But all so soon as the all-cheering sun
Should in the furthest east begin to draw
The shady curtains from Aurora's bed,
Away from the light steals home my heavy son,
And private in his chamber pens himself,
Shuts up his windows, locks far daylight out
And makes himself an artificial night:
Black and portentous must this humour prove,
Unless good counsel may the cause remove.

Benvolio

  My noble uncle, do you know the cause?

Montague

  I neither know it nor can learn of him.

Benvolio

  Have you importuned him by any means?

Montague

  Both by myself and many other friends:
But he, his own affections' counsellor,
Is to himself - I will not say how true -
But to himself so secret and so close,
So far from sounding and discovery,
As is the bud bit with an envious worm,
Ere he can spread his sweet leaves to the air,
Or dedicate his beauty to the sun.
Could we but learn from whence his sorrows grow,
we would as willingly give cure as know.

Enter Romeo

Benvolio

  See, where he comes: so please you, step aside;
I'll know his grievance, or be much denied.

Montague

  I would thou wert so happy by thy stay,
To hear true shrift. Come, madam, let's away.
Exeunt Montague & Lady Montague

Madam, an hour before the sun could be seen in the east (*early in the morning*) I was feeling anxious so I went for a walk; during which - under a grove of sycamore trees which grow on the west side of the city – early in the morning I saw your son: I started to go towards him but he was wary of me and ran away in the shelter of the woods:

I, comparing his feelings with mine, which are very confused when I'm alone, served my own needs by respecting his and gladly let him go, he who ran from me (*Benvolio didn't mind Romeo avoiding him because he wanted to be alone too*).

Many mornings he's been seen there, his tears adding to the morning dew, adding to clouds more clouds with his deep sighs; but as soon as the sun, which cheers everyone up, is in the far east beginning to open the curtains of Aurora's bedroom (*Aurora is the ancient Greek goddess of the dawn*) he runs away from the light to home, my heavy hearted son, and in his bedroom locks himself away, shutting the windows and locking daylight out, making himself an artificial night. This humour of his will show itself to be a bad omen unless some good advice can solve the problem.

My noble uncle, do you know why he is this way?

I do not know it and he will not tell me.

Have you questioned him in some way?

Both I have and many other friends too. But he, acting on his own feelings, is keeping to himself – he probably tells himself all sorts of things – but to himself is so secretive and so closed, so far from being listened to and understood, as is the flower bud when it is bitten by a malicious worm before it can open it's leaves to the air or dedicate it's beauty to the sun. If only we could find out from where his sorrow comes, we would be as ready to help as we are to know [the problem].

Enter Romeo (at a distance).

See, here he comes – if it's okay with you, please leave us; I'll find out what's the matter or be harshly refused.

I hope you are in such a good mood that you'll hear the truth. Come, madam, let's go.

6

Benvolio

   Good-morrow, cousin.

Romeo

   Is the day so young?

Benvolio

   But new struck nine.

Romeo

   Ay me! Sad hours seem long.
      Was that my father that went hence so fast?

Benvolio

   It was. What sadness lengthens Romeo's hours?

Romeo

   Not having that, which, having, makes them short.

Benvolio

   In love?

Romeo

   Out.

Benvolio

   Of love?

Romeo

   Out of her favour, where I am in love.

Benvolio

   Alas, that love, so gentle in his view,
   Should be so tyrannous and rough in proof!

Romeo

   Alas, that love, whose view is muffled still,
   Should, without eyes, see pathways to his will!
   Where shall we dine? O me! What fray was here?
   Yet tell me not, for I have heard it all.
   Here's much to do with hate, but more with love.
   Why, then, O brawling love! O loving hate!
   O any thing, of nothing first create!
   O heavy lightness! serious vanity!
   Mis-shapen chaos of well-seeming forms!
   Feather of lead, bright smoke, cold fire,
   sick health! Still-waking sleep, that is not what it is!
   This love feel I, that feel no love in this.
   Dost thou not laugh?

Benvolio

   No, coz, I rather weep.

Romeo

   Good heart, at what?

Benvolio

   At thy good heart's oppression.

Romeo

   Why, such is love's transgression.
   Griefs of mine own lie heavy in my breast,
   Which thou wilt propagate, to have it prest
   With more of thine: this love that thou hast shown
   Doth add more grief to too much of mine own.
   Love is a smoke raised with the fume of sighs;

[*Good-morrow : good morning*]

Is the time of day so early?

It's just turned nine o'clock.

F me! Sad hours seem long. Was that my father that ran away so quickly?

It was. What is this sadness that makes Romeo's hours so long?

Not having the same thing which if I did have would make them fast.

In love?

Out.

Of love?

Out of her favour, where [*with who*] I am in love.

It's a shame that love, so gentle when you see it, is actually monstrous and rough when actually experienced(*in the proof : first test of a new gun*)!

[*Cupid is meant to have worn a blindfold*] It's a shame that love, who can't see anyway, does, without eyes, find ways to do whatever he likes!... Where should we get some chow [*food*] then? Goodness me! What fight happened here? Wait – don't tell me. I've heard it all before. Here was to do with hate but even this was about love: why then, does love fight? O, loving hate! Or anything which makes something out of nothing! O, heavy lightness! [*he is describing the feeling of love*] Serious vanity! Messed up chaos that looks so nice! Feather as heavy as lead, bright smoke, cold fire, sick health! Still awake when asleep, this thing that is not what it is! This is the love that I feel, the kind of love that feels no love. Do you find something funny?

[*coz: cousin*]

Good man, at what?

At your heart's abuse.

Why, such is love's way of going too far. Griefs of my own are heavy in my breast already and you're trying to make it heavier with weights from your [*propagation : artificially making plants reproduce; Benvolio's concern makes Romeo even more upset*]: the love you show me makes me even more upset. Love is a smoke raised

Being purged, a fire sparkling in lovers' eyes;
Being vex'd a sea nourish'd with lovers' tears:
What is it else? a madness most discreet,
A choking gall and a preserving sweet.
Farewell, my coz.

Benvolio
    Soft! I will go along;
        An if you leave me so, you do me wrong.

Romeo
    Tut, I have lost myself; I am not here;
This is not Romeo, he's some other where.

Benvolio
    Tell me in sadness, who is that you love.

Romeo
    What, shall I groan and tell thee?

Benvolio
    Groan! why, no. But sadly tell me who.

Romeo
    In sadness, cousin, I do love a woman.

Benvolio
    I aim'd so near, when I supposed you loved.

Romeo
    A right good marksman! And she's fair I love.

Benvolio
    A right fair mark, fair coz, is soonest hit.

Romeo
    Well, in that hit you miss: she'll not be hit
With Cupid's arrow; she hath Dian's wit;
And, in strong proof of chastity well arm'd,
From love's weak childish bow she lives unharm'd.
She will not stay the siege of loving terms,
Nor bide the encounter of assailing eyes,
Nor ope her lap to saint-seducing gold:
O, she is rich in beauty, only poor,
That when she dies with beauty dies her store.

Benvolio
    Then she hath sworn that she will still live chaste?

Romeo
    She hath, and in that sparing makes huge waste,
For beauty starved with her severity
Cuts beauty off from all posterity.
She is too fair, too wise, wisely too fair,
To merit bliss by making me despair:
She hath forsworn to love, and in that vow
Do I live dead that live to tell it now.

Benvolio
    Be ruled by me, forget to think of her.

---

with the fume of sighs; once purified it becomes a sparkling fire in the lover's eyes; if it is vexed it becomes a sea made of lover's tears: What else is it? A very discreet madness, a choking poison and a sweet preserver. See you around, 'Cuz.

Hold up! I will go with you and if you duss out on me, you do me wrong.

Hush, I am not myself – I am not here, this person before you is not Romeo, Romeo is somewhere else.

Tell me seriously, who is this girl you're in love with?

What, you want me to groan (*make a big deal out of it*) and tell you?

Groan? Why, no, but seriously tell me who.

In all seriousness, cousin, I do love a woman.

I'd kind of guessed that already.

You're a good shot! And she's beautiful, who I love.

A beautiful target is easier to hit.

Well, on that one you miss: she's not been hit with Cupids arrow; she has Dian's (*Diana : ancient Roman goddess of hunting and virginity*) cunning; And has proven herself to be very chaste. From Love's (*blind Cupid's*) weak and childish bow she has been unharmed. She will not listen to my loving promises, or hold my gaze when our eyes meet, or open her lap for any amount of money: O, she is rich in beauty only it's a shame that when she dies her beauty will die with her, unused.

Then she has taken an oath to stay a virgin?

She has and in that sparing (*of herself from love*) makes a huge waste. For beauty starved by her in this serious way (*Romeo implies that beauty is 'fed' by sexual relations*) means that beauty will never be reproduced (*because she will never have a child to genetically pass on her beauty*). She is too pretty, too wise and wisely too pretty (*she is so beautiful in the mind as well as the body that...*), to earn paradise for herself by making me unhappy (*...she will live without a man's love as best to achieve eternal happiness in heaven*): she has sworn never to fall in love and in that vow do I live dead, creating this person that lives to tell you now.

Listen to me, forget about her, stop thinking about it.

Romeo

O, teach me how I should forget to think.

Benvolio

By giving liberty unto thine eyes;
Examine other beauties.

Romeo

'Tis the way
To call hers exquisite, in question more:
These happy masks that kiss fair ladies' brows
Being black put us in mind they hide the fair;
He that is strucken blind cannot forget
The precious treasure of his eyesight lost:
Show me a mistress that is passing fair,
What doth her beauty serve, but as a note
Where I may read who pass'd that passing fair?
Farewell: thou canst not teach me to forget.

Benvolio

I'll pay that doctrine, or else die in debt.

Exeunt

Oh, teach me how I should forget to think!

By giving freedom to your eyes – look at other beauties.

It's the best way to say how beautiful she is when compared with others: (*back in the day women would wear sheik black masks if they went to the theatre or at some cool parties, supposedly to be modest but often, in fact, to be more promiscuous*) these masks which are held to ladies' faces, being black, make us forget how fine they really are; if someone becomes blind he will never forget the precious treasure of his eyesight lost: show me a mistress who is beautiful and what purpose does her beauty serve other than as a reminder of where I can see a beauty even more beautiful. Goodbye – you cannot teach me to forget.

I'll prove my theory or else die trying.

I.II

Verona's Streets.
Enter Capulet w Servant & Paris

*Another street in Verona. Enter the old Mafia Don **Capulet**, a wealthy young man by the name of **Paris** and a **Servant** attending them.*

Capulet
> But Montague is bound as well as I,
> In penalty alike; and 'tis not hard, I think,
> For men so old as we to keep the peace.

Montague is subject to the same penalty as I am [*the Prince has threatened to execute them if they cannot...*] – it shouldn't be too hard, I think, for old men like us to keep the peace.

Paris
> Of honourable reckoning are you both;
> And pity 'tis you lived at odds so long.
> But now, my lord, what say you to my suit?

You both have reputations for honour and it is a pity that you have lived at odds for so long. But now, what do you say about my proposal?

Capulet
> But saying o'er what I have said before:
> My child is yet a stranger in the world;
> She hath not seen the change of fourteen years.
> Let two more summers wither in their pride,
> Ere we may think her ripe to be a bride.

The same thing I have said before; my child is a still stranger to the [real] world; she has not seen fourteen years pass [*Juliet is still 13 years old*]. Let two more summers [*wither in their... : deteriorate when at their most substantial : turn from hot, bright, golden weather to cold miserable winter*] pass [*ere : before*] we think she's 'ripe' [*ready*] to be a bride.

Paris
> Younger than she are happy mothers made.

Younger than her have been made happy mothers.

Capulet
> And too soon marr'd are those so early made.
> The earth hath swallow'd all my hopes but she,
> She is the hopeful lady of my earth:
> But woo her, gentle Paris, get her heart,
> My will to her consent is but a part;
> An she agree, within her scope of choice
> Lies my consent and fair according voice.
> This night I hold an old accustom'd feast,
> Whereto I have invited many a guest,
> Such as I love; and you, among the store,
> One more, most welcome, makes my number more.
> At my poor house look to behold this night
> Earth-treading stars that make dark heaven light:
> Such comfort as do lusty young men feel
> When well-apparell'd April on the heel
> Of limping winter treads, even such delight
> Among fresh female buds shall you this night
> Inherit at my house; hear all, all see,
> And like her most whose merit most shall be:
> Which on more view, of many mine being one
> May stand in number, though in reckoning none.
> Come, go with me. Go, sirrah, trudge about
> Through fair Verona; find those persons out
> Whose names are written there, and to them say,
> My house and welcome on their pleasure stay.

And too quickly withered out are those who are. Life has crushed all my dreams except her – she is the last hope I have in my world/sole heir [*lady of my earth : fille de terre is a French term for heiress*]. So woo her gently Paris, gain her genuine love [for] my will is only part of the deal, as is her consent. If she agrees, my consent is within the range of her choice.
  Tonight I'm having my old annual party, to which I have invited many guests, who I have love for and you, among them, most welcome, to make those many guests one more. In my little house [*he is joking, he lives in a big mansion*] look around and you will see such beauties that they must be stars walking the earth to make the dark heavens [*because it will be night*] lighter [*because the stars [[beauties]] are not there weighing it down*]. It will be like when April steps on the end of winter, such beautiful fresh female buds [*because women start wearing less clothes in spring and because flowers open their buds*] will you see tonight in my house. Listen to them all, see them all and go for the one you like most: when you've seen so many girls of which my daughter is just one, she may not be able to compete with the others. Come, let's go. [*To Servant:*] Go, sirrah [*sirrah : a term used to address an inferior*], hit the grind on the streets of beautiful Verona and find those persons out that are written there [*referring to list he has given the Servant*] and to them say PARTY AT MY PLACE!!!

> [*Exeunt Capulet and Paris*]

Servant

Find them out whose names are written here!
It is written, that the shoemaker should meddle with
his yard, and the tailor with his last, the fisher with
his pencil, and the painter with his nets; but I am
sent to find those persons whose names are here
writ, and can never find what names the writing
person hath here writ. I must to the learned
                                        -in good time!

Find the people on this list?! It is said that a
shoemaker should work with a tape-measure
and a tailor should work with a ruler [*he is
getting it mixed up*], the fisher with his
paintbrush and the painter with his nets [*clearly
this person is a bit of a doughnut and ill-suited
for the task at hand*]. But here I am, sent to find
these people on this list and I can't read the
names this person has written [*he is illiterate*]. I
must ask someone clever – and quickly too!

Enter Benvolio & Romeo

Benvolio

Tut, man, one fire burns out another's burning,
One pain is lessen'd by another's anguish;
Turn giddy, and be holp by backward turning;
One desperate grief cures with another's languish:
Take thou some new infection to thy eye,
And the rank poison of the old will die.

Come off it mate, one fire goes out and another
starts burning. One pain can be comforted by
another's agony; if you get dizzy from spinning
around, then spin back the other way; one
desperate grief can be cured with another's
misery: take some new infection to your eye [*find
a new woman*] and the rank poison of old will die.

Romeo

Your plaintain-leaf is excellent for that.

[*plantain-leaf: used in bandages for minor or
infected wounds, Romeo is dismissing Benvolio's
idea as a mere plaster*]

Benvolio

For what, I pray thee?

What do I need that for?

Romeo

For your broken shin.

For your broken leg.

Benvolio

Why, Romeo, art thou mad?

Eh, Romeo? Are you mad?

Romeo

Not mad, but bound more than a mad-man is;
Shut up in prison, kept without my food,
Whipp'd and tormented and -God-den, good fellow.

Not mad but confined even more than a madman is; shut up in prison, starved of food,
whipped and tormented and - good evening,
goodfella!

Servant

God gi' god-den. I pray, sir, can you read?

God give you a good evening. Pray you sir, can
you read?

Romeo

Ay, mine own fortune in my misery.

Yes, my own future in my sadness.

Servant

Perhaps you have learned it without book:
but, I pray, can you read any thing you see?

Maybe you've learnt [*your future*] off by heart
[*'maybe you have already decided what your
future will be' or perhaps it is a mistake that the
Servant has made, thinking it is the name of a
poem and Romeo cannot actually read*] but, I
beg you, can you read anything you see?

Romeo

Ay, if I know the letters and the language.

Yes, if I know the letters of the language.

Servant

Ye say honestly: rest you merry!

You are an honest man, farewell! [*apparently the
Servant thinks Romeo cannot read or maybe he
thinks Romeo is messing him about too much
and will not give him a straight answer*] [*also,
isn't that a crazy way of saying goodbye 'rest you
merry' as in 'I hope you die a happy man'?!*]

11

Romeo

Stay, fellow; I can read.
'Signior Martino and his wife and daughters; County
Anselme and his beauteous sisters; the lady widow of
Vitravio; Signior Placentio and his lovely nieces;
Mercutio and his brother Valentine; mine uncle
Capulet, his wife and daughters; my fair niece
Rosaline; Livia; Signior Valentio and his cousin
Tybalt, Lucio and the lively Helena.'
A fair assembly: whither should they come?

Servant

To supper; to our house.

Romeo

Whose house?

Servant

My master's.

Romeo

Indeed, I should have ask'd you that before.

Servant

Now I'll tell you without asking: my master is
the great rich Capulet; and if you be not of the house
of Montagues, I pray, come and crush a cup of wine.
Rest you merry!

[Exit Servant]

Benvolio

At this same ancient feast of Capulet's
Sups the fair Rosaline whom thou so lovest,
With all the admired beauties of Verona:
Go thither; and, with unattainted eye,
Compare her face with some that I shall show,
And I will make thee think thy swan a crow.

Romeo

When the devout religion of mine eye
Maintains such falsehood, then turn tears to fires;
And these, who often drown'd could never die,
Transparent heretics, be burnt for liars!
One fairer than my love! the all-seeing sun
Ne'er saw her match since first the world begun.

Benvolio

Tut, you saw her fair, none else being by,
Herself poised with herself in either eye:
But in that crystal scales let there be weigh'd
Your lady's love against some other maid
That I will show you shining at this feast,
And she shall scant show well that now shows best.

Romeo

I'll go along, no such sight to be shown,
But to rejoice in splendour of mine own.

Exeunt

Stay, my man, I can read.
'Signior Martino and his wife and daughters;
Count Anselme and his beautiful sisters; the lady
widow of Vitravio; Signior Placentio and his lovely
nieces; Mercutio and his brother Valentine; my
uncle Capulet, his wife and daughters; my fair
niece Rosaline; Livia; Signior Valentio and his
cousin Tybalt, Lucio and the lively Helena.'
A good list of important people – where is it they
should come?

Of course, I should have asked you that first (*who
your master is*).

I'll tell you without you having to ask: my master
is the great and rich Capulet and as long as
you're not Montagues, I beg you, come and crack
open a bottle. Farewell!

This feast the Capulet's always have – Rosaline
will be there tonight, who you love, with all the
beauties of Verona: go there and with an
unprejudiced eye compare her face with some
that I will show you and I will make you think your
swan is a crow (*that Rosaline is ugly*).

When the religion of my eyes is corrupted then
turn my tears into fire; and these [eyes], who
often drowned in tears but could never die, will
be seen for heretics (*heretics : people with
highly-controversial, even 'illegal' opinions,
Romeo is saying that his sad eyes will be
branded traitors if his love is proven false by
finding a new desire*) and should be burnt for
being liars! One fairer than my love?! The all-
seeing sun never saw someone as beautiful as
her since the world began.

Pssch! You saw her when no one else was
around, only the image of herself posing in both
eyes. But in those crystal scales let there be
weighed her 'love' against some other maid's
that I will show you shining at this feast and she
won't look so good, she who at the moment looks
like the best.

I'll go along, there's no such woman to be shown,
just a chance for me to rejoice in the amazing
beauty of my own [girl].

I.III

The Capulet Mansion.
Enter Lady Capulet & Nurse

Lady Capulet

    Nurse, where's my daughter? Call her forth to me.

Nurse, where's my daughter? Fetch her for me.

Nurse

    Now, by my maidenhead at twelve year old,
I bade her come. What, lamb! what, ladybird!
God forbid! where's this girl? what, Juliet!

Now then, [*by my maidenhead at twelve year old:*
when the nurse was twelve she was still a virgin
and therefore it was a good thing to swear by...
back then] I told the girl to come here. What,
lamb! What ladybird (*affectionate nicknames*)!
God forbid [something's happened to her]!
Where's that girl? Hello, Juliet!

Enter Juliet

Juliet

    How now! who calls?

What's going on, who's calling for me?

Nurse

    Your mother.

Juliet

    Madam, I am here. What is your will?

Lady Capulet

    This is the matter: - Nurse, give leave awhile,
We must talk in secret: - Nurse, come back again;
I have remember'd me, thou shalt hear our counsel.
Thou know'st my daughter's of a pretty age.

This is the problem – Nurse, please leave us
alone, we must talk in secret – Nurse! Come
back again, I have remembered myself, you are
allowed to listen to our discussion. You know my
daughter is becoming a woman.

Nurse

    Faith, I can tell her age unto an hour.

I swear, I can tell how old she is to the hour.

Lady Capulet

    She's not fourteen?

She's not fourteen?

Nurse

    She is not fourteen. How long is it now
                    To Lammas-tide?

She's not fourteen. How long is it now to the
harvest-time festival?

Lady Capulet

    A fortnight and odd days.

A little over two weeks.

Nurse

    Even or odd, of all days in the year,
Come Lammas-eve at night shall she be fourteen.
Susan and she - God rest all Christian souls! -
Were of an age: well, Susan is with God;
She was too good for me: but, as I said,
On Lammas-eve at night shall she be fourteen;
That shall she, marry; I remember it well.

Roughly a couple of days around all the days of
the year that it is Lammas-eve [*the night before*
the Harvest festival] by the time it is night she
will be fourteen. Susan [*the nurse's own*
daughter] and she [*Juliet*] – God bless all resting
(*deceased*) Christian souls! - were the same
age; well, Susan is with God; she was too good
for me but as I said on Lammas-eve by the time
it is night she will be fourteen; that is the age she
will be, (*marry: I promise*). I remember it well.

Lady Capulet

    Enough of this; I pray thee, hold thy peace. *

Enough of your rambling! Please – stop talking.

    * Nurses' rambling is longer in folios

Nurse

    Yes, madam.

Lady Capulet

        Tell me, daughter Juliet,
How stands your disposition to be married?

Juliet

        It is an honour that I dream not of.

Nurse

        An honour! were not I thine only Nurse,
I would say thou hadst suck'd wisdom from thy teat.

Lady Capulet

        Well, think of marriage now; younger than you,
Here in Verona, ladies of esteem,
Are made already mothers: by my count,
I was your mother much upon these years
That you are now a maid. Thus then in brief:
The valiant Paris seeks you for his love.

Nurse

        A man, young lady! Lady, such a man
As all the world - why, he's a man of wax.

Lady Capulet

        Verona's summer hath not such a flower.

Nurse

        No, he's flower: in faith, a very flower.

Lady Capulet

        What say you? can you love the gentleman?
This night you shall behold him at our feast;
Read o'er the volume of young Paris' face,
And find delight writ there with beauty's pen;
Examine every married lineament,
And see how one another lends content
And what obscured in this fair volume lies
Find written in the margent of his eyes.
This precious book of love, this unbound lover,
To beautify him, only lacks a cover:
The fish lives in the sea; and 'tis much pride
For fair without, the fair within to hide:
That book in many's eyes doth share the glory,
That in gold clasps locks in the golden story;
So shall you share all that he doth possess,
By having him, making yourself no less.

Nurse

        No less! nay, bigger; women grow by men.

Lady Capulet

        Speak briefly, can you like of Paris' love?

Juliet

        I'll look to like, if looking liking move:
But no more deep will I endart mine eye
Than your consent gives strength to make it fly.

     Enter a Servant of Capulet

Tell me, my daughter Juliet, how do you feel about getting married?

It is an honour but something that I currently have no intention of doing.

An honour? If someone else had nursed you I would say you had sucked wisdom from the breasts you fed upon [*but because I was the only one who fed you I am too modest to say that*].

Well, now you can start thinking about getting married; girls younger than you, here in Verona, high-class ladies, have already been made mothers. [*By my count : I reckon*] I gave birth to you around the same age that you are now. So let's cut to the chase; the valiant Paris seeks you for his love.

A real man, young lady! Lady, as good a man as any in the world – why he's the very model of a man.

The city of Verona, in the whole of summertime, doesn't have a flower as pretty as Paris.

No, he's [*not a model*] a flower: Truly, a beautiful flower.

What do you think? Can you love the gentleman? Tonight you will see him at the feast – [*read : look*] over the [*volume : chapter*] of young Paris' face and find happiness written there in beauty's trap. Look at all the harmonious lines [*on his face/'of text'*] and see how they all compliment each other and what you cannot read in his face read in the [*margent : margin*] of his eyes. This precious book of love, this [*unbound : not married / a book printed on pages not bound into an actual book*] lover, in order to make him totally gorgeous he only needs a front cover: [*The fish lives in the sea : 'Paris is still single'*]; and there is great pride for the outwardly beautiful [*woman*] who can contain this beauty [*Paris*]; many people think a book's glory is shared with the golden locket that locks in the golden story; you will share everything he has and so by having him you make yourself no less.

No less! No, you shall be bigger, women grow by men.

Give me an answer quickly – can you love Paris?

I'll try and like him, if looking at him I am moved to: but I will not let my eye be pierced with the arrow of love unless you okay it [*she is being very clever; rather than say 'hell no!' she is saying 'we'll decide together later...'*]

Servant

Madam, the guests are come, supper served up, you called, my young lady asked for, the Nurse cursed in the pantry, and every thing in extremity. I must hence to wait; I beseech you, follow straight.

Madam, the guests have arrived, supper is being served, you have been called for, the young lady (*Juliet*) has been asked for, the nurse is being cursed in the kitchen because she is not there to help serve the food and everything is in chaos. I must go and be a waiter now; I beg you, come with me immediately.

Lady Capulet

We follow thee. Juliet, the county stays.
[Exit Servant & Lady Capulet]

We'll follow you. Juliet, the (*county: Paris is a nobleman with the title of 'county' just like a 'count', for instance, Count Dracula*) is waiting.

Nurse

Go, girl, seek happy nights to happy days.
Exeunt

Go, girl, try and find happy nights and you'll have happy days.

15

I.IV

Verona's streets, at night.
Enter Romeo, Mercutio, Benvolio,
w five or six maskers,
torch-bearers & others

Romeo
What, shall this speech be spoke for our excuse?
Or shall we on without a apology?

Benvolio
The date is out of such prolixity:
We'll have no Cupid hoodwink'd with a scarf,
Bearing a Tartar's painted bow of lath,
Scaring the ladies like a crow-keeper;
Nor no without-book prologue, faintly spoke
After the prompter, for our entrance:
But let them measure us by what they will;
We'll measure them a measure, and be gone.

Romeo
Give me a torch: I am not for this ambling;
Being but heavy, I will bear the light.
Mercutio
Nay, gentle Romeo, we must have you dance.
Romeo
Not I, believe me: you have dancing shoes
With nimble soles: I have a soul of lead
So stakes me to the ground I cannot move.

Mercutio
You are a lover; borrow Cupid's wings,
And soar with them above a common bound.
Romeo
I am too sore enpierced with his shaft
To soar with his light feathers, and so bound,
I cannot bound a pitch above dull woe:
Under love's heavy burden do I sink.
Mercutio
And, to sink in it, should you burden love;
Too great oppression for a tender thing.
Romeo
Is love a tender thing? It is too rough,
Too rude, too boisterous and it pricks like thorn.
Mercutio
If love be rough with you, be rough with love;
Prick love for pricking, and you beat love down.
Give me a case to put my visage in:
A visor for a visor!

Mercutio is Romeo's crazy friend (You have been warned: Mercutio is one crazy s-o-b). We already know Benvolio from the first scene. They are rolling with a bunch of jokers in masks, people holding old-school 'fire' torches and 'others', presumably meaning girls as they definitely arrive with some in the next scene; They are on their way to the Capulet's masked ball.

What, will we use this speech as a kind of excuse? Or do we just go walk up in the party without an apology?

These days people don't bother with such courtesies [*i.e. introducing yourself*]; we won't have some wannabe Cupid, wearing a blindfold made from a scarf, walking around with a [*Tartar : ancient Eastern warrior*]'s bow made of [*lath : thin measure of wood*], scaring the ladies like a scarecrow; Nor no memorized story, said in a low voice, prompting each other on our way in. Let them make of us what they will. We'll do a little dance with them and then be gone [*a measure : any old well-known dance routine*].

Give me a torch – I don't want to get mixed up in this song and dance; I'm feeling down so I will [pretend to be one of our torch-bearers].

No, gentle Romeo, you have to dance with us!

Not I, believe me: you have dancing shoes with lively soles [*the bottom of a shoe / having a hearty soul is also essential for a good dance*]: I have a soul of lead and it pins me to the ground so that I cannot move.

You are a romantic – borrow Cupid's wings and soar with them above the dance.

I am too deeply pierced [*by Cupid*] with his arrow to soar with his light feathers and so wrapped-up that I cannot even jump a little bit above dull woe. Under love's heavy burden, I sink.

If you sink in it then you will make love heavy – too much of a drag for such a delicate thing.

If love be rough with you, be rough with love! Prick love for pricking and you beat love down. Give me a case to put my facial expression in: A visor [*in the sense that a grumpy facial expression is like a visor*] for a visor [*in the*

>   *What care I*
> *what curious eye doth quote deformities?*
> *Here are the beetle brows shall blush for me.*

sense that he is now putting on a real mask for the Capulet's *'Masked Ball'*)! What do I care what curious eye notices my troubles? Here (*on his mask*) are eyebrows that will blush (*make Romeo look like he is having a good time/is attracted to someone*) for me (*because the mask will hide Romeo's true gloomy expression*).

Benvolio

>   *Come, knock and enter; and no sooner in,*
> *But every man betake him to his legs.*

Come, knock and enter – the second we're in there every man is free to follow his legs [wherever or whatever they tell him to do].

Romeo

>   *A torch for me: let wantons light of heart*
> *Tickle the senseless rushes with their heels,*
> *For I am proverb'd with a grandsire phrase;*
> *I'll be a candle-holder, and look on.*
> *The game was ne'er so fair and I am done.*

I want to be a torch-bearer: let thrill-seekers who are in a good mood (*Tickle the... : 1. humour their sudden urges with their feet by dancing 2. Rushes ([Juncaceae reeds]) where strewn on the floor before carpets where invented*). I'm gonna stick with an old phrase my grandad used to say; I'll be a good candle-holder and look on (*'A good candle holder proves a good gamester' - old English proverb meaning the person who watches others play a game will learn to play the game very well himself*). Because the game was never so fair (*because I have found this perfect girl Rosaline*) I'll quit while I'm ahead.

Mercutio

>   *Tut, dun's the mouse, the constable's own word:*
> *If thou art dun, we'll draw thee from the mire*
> *Of this 'save-reverence' love, wherein thou stick'st*
> *Up to the ears. Come, we burn daylight, ho!*

Pshh! Quiet as a mouse, sitting around doing nothing like a policeman?! If you are done then we'll pull you up from the bog of this 'sugar honey iced-tea' love, which you are stuck in up to the ears. Come, we're not burning fire, we're burning daylight (*wasting time*)!

Romeo

>   *Nay, that's not so.*

(*Romeo thinks his love genuine*).

Mercutio

>   *I mean, sir, in delay*
> *We waste our lights in vain, like lamps by day.*
> *Take our good meaning, for our judgement sits*
> *Five times in that ere once in our five wits.*

(*Mercutio deliberately misunderstands him;*) I mean, sir, in wasting time we waste our torches for nothing, like lamps in the day. Take it for a good meaning for when we show good judgement it is five times more the amount than if we used our other five wits just once (*Shakespeare's ' five wits ' are common sense, fantasy, imagination, estimation and memory*).

Romeo

>   *And we mean well in going to this mask;*
> *   But 'tis no wit to go.*

We have good intentions going to this masked ball but it is not good judgement to go.

Mercutio

>   *Why, may one ask?*

Romeo

>   *I dream'd a dream to-night.*

Mercutio

>   *And so did I.*

Romeo

>   *Well, what was yours?*

Mercutio

>   *That dreamers often lie.*

That dreams often lie.

Romeo

>   *In bed asleep, while they do dream things true.*

In bed asleep (*'lying' in bed*), while they do dream things that are true.

Mercutio

O, then, I see Queen Mab hath been with you.
She is the fairies' midwife, and she comes
In shape no bigger than an agate-stone
On the fore-finger of an alderman,
Drawn with a team of little atomies
Athwart men's noses as they lie asleep;
Her wagon-spokes made of long spiders' legs,
The cover of the wings of grasshoppers,
The traces of the smallest spider's web,
The collars of the moonshine's watery beams,
Her whip of cricket's bone, the lash of film,
Her wagoner a small grey-coated gnat,
Not so big as a round little worm
Prick'd from the lazy finger of a maid;
Her chariot is an empty hazel-nut
Made by the joiner squirrel or old grub,
Time out o' mind the fairies' coachmakers.
And in this state she gallops night by night
Through lovers' brains, and then they dream of love;
O'er courtiers' knees, that dream on court'sies
                                                    straight,
   O'er lawyers' fingers, who straight dream on fees,
O'er ladies ' lips, who straight on kisses dream,
Which oft the angry Mab with blisters plagues,
Because their breaths with sweetmeats tainted are:
Sometime she gallops o'er a courtier's nose,
And then dreams he of smelling out a suit;
And sometime comes she with a tithe-pig's tail
Tickling a parson's nose as a' lies asleep,
Then dreams, he of another benefice:
Sometime she driveth o'er a soldier's neck,
And then dreams he of cutting foreign throats,
Of breaches, ambuscadoes, Spanish blades,
Of healths five-fathom deep; and then anon
Drums in his ear, at which he starts and wakes,
And being thus frighted swears a prayer or two
And sleeps again. This is that very Mab
That plats the manes of horses in the night,
And bakes the elflocks in foul sluttish hairs,
Which once untangled, much misfortune bodes:
This is the hag, when maids lie on their backs,
That presses them and learns them first to bear,
Making them women of good carriage:
This is she -

O, then I see Queen Mab has been with you [*Queen Mab: a crazy fictional character cooked up by Mercutio possibly referring to the ancient word 'madb' for 'mead' which would make a strong alcoholic drink resulting in deep sleep*]! She is the fairies' midwife [*she is the nurse present when dreams are born*] and she is smaller than the engraved stone on a ring of the finger of a elderly government official, she comes with a team of little minions as small as atoms and goes up men's noses as they lie asleep; her carriage has wagon-wheels made of spider's legs, a cover made of the wings of grasshoppers, the ropes made of the smallest spider's webs, harnesses made of moonshine's watery beams; her whip is made of cricket's bone, the lash made of gossamer; Her wagon driver is a little insect in a grey-coat, not even as big as the little worms that grow in unmarried women's blood. Her chariot is an empty hazel-nut made by a carpenter who is a squirrel or an old beetle, since before time the fairies have been coach-makers. And in this fashion she gallops nightly through lover's brains and then they dream of love; galloping over men of the courts' knees then they dream of bowing, over lawyers' fingers, who then dream of their fees, over ladies' lips so they dream of kisses which often the angry Queen Mab hurts with blisters because their breath is tainted with candy. Sometimes she gallops over a promoter's nose and then he dreams of smelling out his clients. Sometimes she comes with a [*tithe-pig: pig intended for payment*]'s tail and tickles a person's nose as they lie asleep and then they dream of having a second job. Sometimes she drives over a soldier's neck and then he dreams of cutting foreign throats, of [*breaches: busting into the enemy camp*], of ambushes, Spanish swords [*Toldeo, Spain was famous for making the best swords in 15th-17th centuries*], of toasts five-fathoms deep [*a hell of a lot of wine*] and then soon he hears drums in his ear, at which he starts and wakes up and being thus upset swears a prayer or two and sleeps again. This is that very Queen Mab that braids the manes of horses in the night [*elves are responsible for matted fur on animals and will take revenge if it is ruffled*] and who tangles up human hair in the night so that it is messy and sluttish [*actually, there was a real disease called Plica Polonica but the superstitious belief mischievous faeries were at work was a genuine fear of the times*], which once untangled brings bad luck: this is the hag, when maids are lying down sleeping, that presses them and teaches them to bear heavy weights [*like men or pregnancy*]. This is she -

18

Romeo

    Peace, peace, Mercutio, peace!
Thou talk'st of nothing.

Alright, alright, Mercutio, shut-up! You're talking air.

Mercutio

    True, I talk of dreams,
Which are the children of an idle brain,
Begot of nothing but vain fantasy,
Which is as thin of substance as the air
And more inconstant than the wind, who wooes
Even now the frozen bosom of the north,
And, being anger'd, puffs away from thence,
Turning his face to the dew-dropping south.

True, I talk of dreams, which are the children of a lazy brain, gotten by no way but fantasy, which is as thin in substance as the air and which are more erratic than the winds, which are even at this very moment frozen in the north and being angered by all this puffs away from there turning his efforts to the south [*like a lover jumping from one person to the next*].

Benvolio

    This wind, you talk of, blows us from ourselves;
Supper is done, and we shall come too late.

This wind you talk of is now delaying us further – supper is finished and if we don't get going we'll be late.

Romeo

    I fear, too early: for my mind misgives
Some consequence yet hanging in the stars
Shall bitterly begin his fearful date
With this night's revels and expire the term
Of a despised life closed in my breast
By some vile forfeit of untimely death.
But He, that hath the steerage of my course,
Direct my sail! On, lusty gentlemen.

I'm afraid we'll get there too early for my mind suspects some event is waiting in the stars and it will bitterly [*begin it's fearful date: 'start it's dreadful process', 'begin it's awful term'*] with this night's adventure and will finish my hated life [*he 'hates' his life because he is not with Rosaline*] – this knowledge I can feel in my heart - by some horrible trick of untimely death. But God, that steers my course, direct my sail! On, raunchy gentlemen!

Benvolio

    Strike, drum.

        Exeunt

[*The attendants are playing music; now that's a cool way to show up at a party, with your own entourage playing a theme tune on the way in!*]

The / I talk of dreams

I.V

A Hallway of the Capulet Mansion.
Musicians waiting. Enter Servants

First Servant

Where's Potpan, that he helps not to take away?
He shift a trencher! He scrape a trencher!

Second Servant

When good manners shall lie all in one or two
men's hands and they unwashed too, 'tis a foul thing.

First Servant

Away with the joint-stools, remove the
court-cupboard, look to the plate: - good thou, save
me a piece of marchpane; and, as thou lovest me, let
the porter let in Susan Grindstone and Nell. -
Antony and Potpan!

Second Servant

Ay, boy, ready.

First Servant

You are looked for and called for, asked for and
sought for, in the great chamber.

Second Servant

We cannot be here and there too. Cheerly, boys;
be brisk awhile and the longer liver take all.

[Exit First & Second Servant]

Enter Capulet w Juliet and others of his house,
meeting the guests and maskers

Capulet

Welcome, gentlemen! ladies that have their toes
Unplagued with corns will walk a bout with you.
Ah ha, my mistresses! which of you all
Will now deny to dance? she that makes dainty,
She, I'll swear, hath corns; am I come near ye now?
Welcome, gentlemen! I have seen the day
That I have worn a visor and could tell
A whispering tale in a fair lady's ear,
Such as would please: 'tis gone, 'tis gone, 'tis gone:
You are welcome, gentlemen! come, musicians, play.
A hall, a hall! give room, and foot it, girls.
[Music plays and they dance merrily]
More light, you knaves; and turn the tables up,
And quench the fire, the room is grown too hot.
Ah, sirrah, this unlook'd-for sport comes well.
Nay, sit, nay, sit, good cousin Capulet;
For you and I are past our dancing days:
How long is't now since last yourself and I
Were in a mask?

We now enter the party. 'Musicians waiting'
really means the roof is on fyah!!

Where's that Potpan fella, not helping us clear
the plates? He supposed to shift a plate [*clear
the tables*] then scrape a plate!

When good manners are only left in a couple of
men's hands, and even they're unwashed
[*'getting their hands dirty'*], it's a terrible thing.

Take away the hand-made stools, remove the
side board, look to the silverware. - good as you
are, save me a piece of marzipan [*marchpane :
filberts, almonds, pistachios, pine-kernels, sugar
of roses and a little flour*] and because you love
me, tell the gatekeeper to let Susan Grindstone
and Nell into the party. - Antony and Potpan!

Yes, boy, ready.

You are being looked and called for, asked and
sought for, in the main hall.

We can't be here and there too. Cheerfully boys,
be quick for a while, he who lives longest gets it
all [*old proverb meaning live for the day because
the longer you live the more bull**** you have
to put up with*]

Enter Capulet with Juliet and others from the
same click, welcoming the guests and people
wearing masks.

[*-addressing Romeo & Co. !!*]
Welcome gentlemen! Ladies that have not tired
out their feet will have a dance with you. Ah ha,
my mistresses! Which of you will refuse to
dance? She that is too timid to do so, I swear,
has corns on her feet; do I know what I'm on
about? Welcome gentlemen! I remember the
days when I wore a mask and could whisper a
few tales in a beautiful girl's ear, such as she
would like: but it's gone now, it's gone, it's gone!
You are welcome gentlemen! Come, DJ, play on!
[*A hall! A hall! : 'Make way! Make way!'*], make
some room! Give room and show us what you've
got girls!
     More light, you knaves! And turn the tables
up [*all tables were boards, Capulet instructs
them to fold the tables away to make room for
dancing*], and turn the heat down, the room is
getting too hot! Ah, sirrah [*sirrah & knave:
condescending forms of address often used
when talking to an inferior/servant/man on
road*] this unexpected excitement is great. Hey,
sit down good cousin Capulet [*talking to his
cousin, another Capulet*]; for you and I are past
the days when we could dance; how long is it
now since you and I were last wearing masks?

Second Capulet
>   By'r lady, thirty years.

By Mother Mary, thirty years.

Capulet
>   What, man! 'tis not so much, 'tis not so much:
>   'Tis since the nuptials of Lucentio,
>   Come Pentecost as quickly as it will,
>   Some five and twenty years; and then we mask'd.

What man? It isn't that much, it isn't that much: it was since the wedding of Lucentio, so come Pentecost (*the seventh Sunday after Easter*) it will be about twenty five years since we masked.

Second Capulet
>   'Tis more, 'tis more, his son is elder, sir;
>   His son is thirty.

It's more, it's more – his son is elder sir, his son is thirty.

Capulet
>   Will you tell me that?
>   His son was but a ward two years ago.

Are you sure about that? His son was still living at home two years ago.

Romeo [To a Servingman]
>   What lady is that, which doth enrich the hand
>   Of yonder knight?

(*Asking a waiter:*) What woman is that, who does make wonderful the hand of that knight over there?

Servant
>   I know not, sir.

Romeo
>   O, she doth teach the torches to burn bright!
>   It seems she hangs upon the cheek of night
>   Like a rich jewel in an Ethiope's ear;
>   Beauty too rich for use, for earth too dear!
>   So shows a snowy dove trooping with crows,
>   As yonder lady o'er her fellows shows.
>   The measure done, I'll watch her place of stand,
>   And, touching hers, make blessed my rude hand.
>   Did my heart love till now? forswear it, sight!
>   For I ne'er saw true beauty till this night.

Oh, she does show the torches how to burn brighter! It seems she hangs upon the cheek of night like a rich jewel in an Ethiopian's ear; beauty too expensive to be used, for earth too dear! So it is when a snow white dove rolls with crows as this lady over there over her fellow peopledem shows. When the dance is over I'll see where she goes and by touching hers, make my rough hand blessed. Did my heart love before now? I can't believe my eyes! For I never saw true beauty until this night.

Tybalt
>   This, by his voice, should be a Montague.
>   Fetch me my rapier, boy. What dares the slave
>   Come hither, cover'd with an antic face,
>   To fleer and scorn at our solemnity?
>   Now, by the stock and honour of my kin,
>   To strike him dead, I hold it not a sin.

(*some distance away from Romeo:*)
I can tell by his voice, this is a Montague. Get me a sword, boy. How dare this slave comes here, covered with his grotesque mask to mock and scorn at our ceremony? Now, by my family-line and for the honour of my crew, to strike him dead I wouldn't consider a sin.

Capulet
>   Why, how now, kinsman! wherefore storm you so?

Why, what's the matter family? Where are you storming off to?

Tybalt
>   Uncle, this is a Montague, our foe,
>   A villain that is hither come in spite,
>   To scorn at our solemnity this night.

Uncle, this is a Montague, our enemy, a villain that has come here in spite to scorn at our festivity tonight.

Capulet
>   Young Romeo is it?

Tybalt
>   'Tis he, that villain Romeo.

It's him, that villain Romeo.

Capulet
>   Content thee, gentle coz, let him alone;
>   He bears him like a portly gentleman;
>   And, to say truth, Verona brags of him
>   To be a virtuous and well-govern'd youth:
>   I would not for the wealth of all the town

Chill your skin, gentle cousin and leave him alone; he is conducting himself like a well-mannered gentleman and to be truthful, Verona speaks of him to be a virtuous and well-disciplined youth: I would not for all the money in town

Here in my house do him disparagement:
Therefore be patient, take no note of him:
It is my will, the which if thou respect,
Show a fair presence and put off these frowns,
An ill-beseeming semblance for a feast.

Tybalt
It fits, when such a villain is a guest:
I'll not endure him.

Capulet
He shall be endured:
What, goodman boy! I say, he shall: go to;
Am I the master here, or you? go to.
You'll not endure him? God shall mend my soul!
You'll make a mutiny among my guests!
You will set cock-a-hoop! You'll be the man!

Tybalt
Why, uncle, 'tis a shame.

Capulet
Go to, go to; You are a saucy boy: is't so, indeed?
This trick may chance to scathe you, I know what.
Well said, my hearts! You are a princox; go:
Be quiet, or - More light, more light! - for shame
I'll make you quiet. What, cheerly, my hearts!

Tybalt
Patience perforce with wilful choler meeting
Makes my flesh tremble in their different greeting.
I will withdraw: but this intrusion shall
Now seeming sweet convert to bitter gall.
[Exit Tybalt]

Romeo [To Juliet]
If I profane with my unworthiest hand
This holy shrine, the gentle fine is this:
My lips, two blushing pilgrims, ready stand
To smooth that rough touch with a tender kiss.

Juliet
Good pilgrim, you do wrong your hand too much,
Which mannerly devotion shows in this;
For saints have hands that pilgrims' hands do touch,
And palm to palm is holy palmers' kiss.

Romeo
Have not saints lips, and holy palmers too?

Juliet
Ay, pilgrim, lips that they must use in prayer.

Romeo
O, then, dear saint, let lips do what hands do;
They pray, grant thou, lest faith turn to despair.

Juliet
Saints do not move, though grant for prayers' sake.

---

disrespect him here in my house. Therefore be patient, take no notice of him. It is my will, which if you respect, be friendly and stop frowning, it's an inappropriate (*semblance: way of looking*) for a party.

I *should* look so angry when such a villain is a guest: I'll not put up with him.

He will be put up with! What, you middle-class teenager?! I say he will be endured so go on, get. Am I the master here or you? Go to. You'll not endure him? God save me! You'll make a riot among my guests! You're just trying to make a name for yourself! You wanna be a big man yeah?

Why, uncle, it's a shame.

Go to, go to – you are an impertinent boy! Is it a shame indeed? This stupidity might end up getting you into serious trouble, I know what [the f I'm talking about]. (*addressing passers-by, trying to look like everything's cool...*) Well said, my friends! (*Back to Tybalt again:*) You are an insolent boy, go, be quiet or – More light! More light! - for shame I'll make you quiet.

Self-restraint meeting with furious anger makes my flesh tremble in their different greetings. I'll bounce - but this intrusion that looks so sweet now will be turned into bitter poison.

(*taking her by the hand*)
If I desecrate, with my unworthy hand, this holy shrine, the gentle penalty is this: my lips, like two blushing pilgrims stand ready to smooth the rough touch (*of my hand*) with a tender kiss.

Good pilgrim, there's no need for that, your hand is already reverent in that it is holding mine; for saints have hands that pilgrims hands do touch and palm to palm (*play on words, palm in the sense of human hands but also as in a pilgrim might bring back palm leaves from the Holy Land*) is the holy palmer's kiss.
Don't saints and holy men have lips too?

Oh then, dear saint, let lips do what hands were meant for. They pray, you must agree, to prevent faith turning into despair.

Saints cannot do that (*keep someone's faith up*) although they might grant wishes made in prayer.

Romeo

Then move not, while my prayer's effect I take.
Thus from my lips, by yours, my sin is purged.

[Romeo kisses Juliet]

Juliet

Then have my lips the sin that they have took!

Romeo

Sin from thy lips? O trespass sweetly urged!
Give me my sin again.

[Juliet kisses Romeo]

Juliet

You kiss by the book.

Nurse

Madam, your mother craves a word with you.

Romeo

What is her mother?

Nurse

Marry, bachelor,
Her mother is the lady of the house,
And a good lady, and a wise and virtuous.
I nursed her daughter, that you talk'd withal;
I tell you, he that can lay hold of her
Shall have the chinks.

Romeo

Is she a Capulet? O dear account!
My life is my foe's debt.

Benvolio

Away, begone; the sport is at the best.

Romeo

Ay, so I fear; the more is my unrest.

Capulet

Nay, gentlemen, prepare not to be gone;
We have a trifling foolish banquet towards.
Is it e'en so? why, then, I thank you all
I thank you, honest gentlemen; good night.
More torches here! Come on then, let's to bed.
Ah, sirrah, by my fay, it waxes late:
I'll to my rest.

[Exit Capulet, carried off by Servant]

Juliet

Come hither, nurse. What is yond gentleman?

Nurse

The son and heir of old Tiberio.

Juliet

What's he that now is going out of door?

Nurse

Marry, that, I think, be young Petrucio.

Juliet

What's he that follows there, that would not dance?

Nurse

I know not.

Then stay still while I make a wish. Thus from me praying, by your instruction, my sin is purged.

Then my lips now possess the sin taken from yours!

Sin from my lips? Oh, sin that is sweetly pushed on! Give me back my sin.

Madam, your mother wants a word with you.

Who is her mother?

By Mary, young man, her mother is the lady of the house and a good lady and wise and virtuous [one]. I nursed her daughter, that you talked with and I'm telling you, he that can hold her down will have lots of money and a great time.

Is she a Capulet? Oh that was expensive! My life is in the hands of my enemy.

Let's go – the games are their peak.

Yes, so I fear – this upsets me (*because he may never see Juliet again*).

No, gentlemen, don't get ready to go! We have some refreshments coming. What, you really must go? Why, then, I thank you all, I thank you, honest gentlemen, good night. More torches here! Come on then, let's get to bed. Ah, sirrah, by my faith it's starting to get late: I'm going to have a rest.

Come here, nurse. Who is that gentlemen over there?

And who's that going out of the door?

I swear, I think that's young Petrucio.

And who's he that's walking over there who would not dance?

Juliet

> Go ask his name: if he be married.
> My grave is like to be my wedding bed.

Go ask his name: if he's married, my grave is likely to be the only thing I will be getting into bed with (*she will die a virgin if she can't have Romeo*).

Nurse

> His name is Romeo, and a Montague;
> The only son of your great enemy.

(*The Nurse knew exactly who he was*)

Juliet

> My only love sprung from my only hate!
> Too early seen unknown, and known too late!
> Prodigious birth of love it is to me,
> That I must love a loathed enemy.

My only love has come from my only hate! I saw him too early when I didn't know him and now I know him, it's too late! Portentous (*'ominous forecast', 'menacing omen'*) birth of love it seems to me that I must love a hated enemy.

Nurse

> What's this? what's this?

What do you mean? What are you talking about?

Juliet

> A rhyme I learn'd even now
> Of one I danced withal.
> [*One calls within for Juliet*]

A rhyme I learnt just now from a person I danced with.

Nurse

> Anon, anon!
> Come, let's away; the strangers all are gone.
> *Exeunt*

Commentary : Act I

Sampson & Gregory are an odd couple. They walk a fine line between hyped-up mega-goons looking for the fight of their lives and yellow-bellied wimps afraid of just about everything, including each other. Whatever the balance, they certainly break all hell loose and for any one who's seen Franco Zeffirelli's film *Romeo and Juliet, 1968* the mayhem that ensues will not have escaped you. Food being hurled everywhere, the whole town diving head first into a mid-afternoon brawl, bells ringing, market stalls getting knocked over, women and children joining the fray and whopping great punching sound effects that would put Batman to shame – it's like my prep school was on a good day.

Emerging from the rubble, Benvolio attempts to reconcile Romeo and the reason for his friend's recent dejection becomes quite clear; unrequited love or rather, one-sided, self-induced infatuation. Shakespeare introduces Romeo by serving him up on a silver platter for ridicule and we, the hungry audience, greedily devour him: he is naïve, he is pathetic, he is charming, he is a puppy with big round sad eyes, moaning for a treat that we can't give him and for the meantime at least, we don't even want to.

Somehow - and this is indeed where these stories often lead us in real life - Benvolio talks him into gatecrashing this huuuuge craaazzzy party and Romeo reluctantly agrees. En route to the Capulet's Mansion we meet Mercutio, who to say is 'mad' would be a serious understatement. The Queen Mab speech is almost capable of making us feel intoxicated as we listen to Mercutio rambling on and on and on, pushing the phrase 'taking a joke too far' to whole new stratospheres of meaning. A detail that Baz Lurnham quite clearly deliberately copied or referenced in his own film *Romeo + Juliet, 1996* from Zeffirelli's version, was that by the end of this speech Mercutio isn't even entertaining his friends any more but has gone off the rails, lost in his own whirlwind of passion, forgetting time and place in his vehement prosecution of the wickedly mischievous fairies' midwife. When Romeo goes to calm him and bring him back down to earth, saying *"Mercutio, peace! Thou talk'st of nothing!"* Mercutio coolly replies *"True, I talk of dreams, which are the children of an idle brain, begot of nothing but vain fantasy,"* turning Romeo's sentiment on himself, as he must now concede his own dreams are no more valid a reason to stay behind than Mercutio's are to get him wound up like that. Whatever Romeo's dream was, thanks to Mercutio, we'll never know, but a moment later amid the furious comedy unfolding a thundering rumble tells of a distant storm brewing as Romeo says *"...my mind misgives some consequence yet hanging in the stars shall begin his fearful date with this night's revels and expire the term of a despised life closed in my breast by some vile forfeit of untimely death."* And then, considering his reluctance to even go to the party at all in the beginning of the scene, Romeo commits to his fate and plunges himself head-first into his tragic destiny proclaiming *"But He* [God]*, that hath the steerage of my course, direct my sail! On, lusty gentlemen!"*

It doesn't take long before the music goes quiet and in slow-motion he witnesses Juliet spinning on the dance-floor, a radiant angel that 'teaches the torches to burn bright'. Nowhere in the play is the plain stupidity of youthful love better pronounced than here; Romeo doesn't even know her name, for all he knows she might be a total bitch, his desire purely sexual as there is no capacity yet introduced for an intellectual appreciation of her character. But no matter what 'the facts' may be, her beauty inspires such a magical sense of wonder in him that we, like Romeo, put our tempered sensibilities aside for one-flipping-moment and share in his amazement at the sparkling grace of a woman's beauty.

Apparently Romeo is pretty easy on the eyes too and makes short work of his bride-to-be, jumping on her and kissing her a matter of seconds after he announces to her his existence in the world. Thrusting himself forward, squeezing her hand, flattering her with eloquent and romantic language, kissing her without express permission, watching her get swept away by the Nurse – this is what young girls really want; a hot, gentle, young man desperate to be close with them, infused with the spice of mystery and a good measure of sincerity to complete the effect. 'Love at first sight' is what we usually call it but in the sceptical, marriage-hopping society we live in today the seriousness of what we are observing might escape us; as much as we might raise our eyebrows at Romeo's sudden lusty desire we must also remember he is intending, and quite genuinely so, to spend the rest of his life with this girl he has only just seen. He is aware of the same things we are – even then people had sex the whole time without getting married – but Romeo, Romeo is a hopeless romantic and in the next few hours of his life his future will be sealed as assuredly as his uncompromising dedication to Juliet. So don't get it twisted; this really is *LOVE* at first sight.

ACT II

A side-street,
that runs along Capulet's orchard.
Enter Romeo

Romeo

    Can I go forward when my heart is here?
    Turn back, dull earth, and find thy centre out.

Can I go forward when my heart is trapped here? Turn back, my body, which is like dull earth, and find your centre [*Juliet is the centre of Romeo's world*].

    He climbeth the wall and leaps down within it.
    Enter Benvolio & Mercutio

Benvolio

    Romeo! my cousin Romeo!

Mercutio

                   He is wise;
    And, on my li' hath stol'n him home to bed.

He is wise and on my life has run home to bed.

Benvolio

    He ran this way and leap'd this orchard wall:
Call, good Mercutio.

He ran this way and leaped over this orchard wall. Call for him, good Mercutio.

Mercutio

              Nay, I'll conjure too.
Romeo! humours! madman! passion! lover!
Appear thou in the likeness of a sigh:
Speak but one rhyme, and I am satisfied;
Cry but 'Ay me!' pronounce but 'love' and 'dove;'
Speak to my gossip Venus one fair word,
One nick-name for her purblind son and heir,
Young Abraham Cupid, he that shot so trim,
When King Cophetua loved the beggar-maid!
He heareth not, he stirreth not, he moveth not;
The ape is dead, and I must conjure him.
I conjure thee by Rosaline's bright eyes,
By her high forehead and her scarlet lip,
By her fine foot, straight leg and quivering thigh
And the demesnes that there adjacent lie,
That in thy likeness thou appear to us!

Nay, I'll raise his spirit up too! Romeo! Dreamer! Madman! Passionate one! Lover! Appear before us like a sigh, speak two sentences to let us know you're okay and I will be satisfied; just shout out 'Yes, me!' say 'love' and 'dove', speak to my gossip Venus [*the goddess of love*] one nice word, one nick-name for her dim-sighted son and heir Young Abraham Cupid, he that shot so accurately when King Cophetua [*this is a reference to an old medieval romance called 'The King and the Beggar-maid' similar to My Fair Lady*] loved the beggar-maid! [*Now talking about Romeo to Benvolio:*] He can't hear, he doesn't stir and he doesn't move; the ape [*affectionate term for young men and perhaps a reference to the fact he is hiding in the trees*] is dead and I must bring him back to life. I summon you by Rosaline's bright eyes, by her high forehead and her scarlet lip, by her fine foot, straight leg and quivering thigh and all the estates and grounds that are next to her/she is next in line for, that in your likeness you will appear to us [*'in your likeness' because he is jokingly addressing a ghost as though in a séance*]!

Benvolio

    And if he hear thee, thou wilt anger him.

If he hears you, that's gonna piss him off.

Mercutio

    This cannot anger him: 'twould anger him
To raise a spirit in his mistress' circle
Of some strange nature, letting it there stand
Till she had laid it and conjured it down;
That were some spite: my invocation
Is fair and honest, and in his mistress' name
I conjure only but to raise up him.

That couldn't anger him: it would anger him to raise a strange spirit in his mistress' name, then let it stand here until she had put it to rest [*because Romeo will not reveal himself and satisfy the spirit they are joking about*]. That would be a piss-take: my spell is fair and honest and in his mistress' name I conjure only but to raise him up.

Benvolio

Come, he hath hid himself among these trees,
To be consorted with the humorous night:
Blind is his love and best befits the dark.

Mercutio

If love be blind, love cannot hit the mark.
Now will he sit under a medlar tree,
And wish his mistress were that kind of fruit.
Romeo, that she were, O, that she were
An open et caetera, thou a poperin pear!
Romeo, good night: I'll to my truckle-bed;
This field-bed is too cold for me to sleep:
Come, shall we go?

Benvolio

Go, then; for 'tis in vain
To seek him here that means not to be found.

Exeunt

Come, he has hidden himself among these trees to be associated with the [*humourous : humid, the air is hot and thick*] night. Blind is his love and it goes well with the dark.

If love is blind, love cannot hit the mark. Now he'll sit under a [*medlar: a rare African fruit*] tree and wish his mistress were that kind of fruit. Romeo, that she were, oh, that she were an open fruit and you a [*poperin pear : a pear of phallic shape*]! Romeo, good night, I'll to my bunk bed, this 'field bed' is too cold for me to sleep in: come, shall we go?

Let's go then, for it's pointless trying to find him here when he doesn't want to be found.

II.II

Capulet's Orchard.
Enter Romeo

Romeo

> *He jests at scars that never felt a wound.*
> *[Juliet appears above at a window]*
> *But, soft! what light through yonder window breaks?*
> *It is the east, and Juliet is the sun!*
> *Arise, fair sun, and kill the envious moon,*
> *Who is already sick and pale with grief,*
> *That thou her maid art far more fair than she:*
> *Be not her maid, since she is envious;*
> *Her vestal livery is but sick and green*
> *And none but fools do wear it; cast it off.*
> *It is my lady, O, it is my love!*
> *O, that she knew she were!*
> *She speaks yet she says nothing: what of that?*
> *Her eye discourses; I will answer it.*
> *I am too bold, 'tis not to me she speaks:*
> *Two of the fairest stars in all the heaven,*
> *Having some business, do entreat her eyes*
> *To twinkle in their spheres till they return.*
> *What if her eyes were there, they in her head?*
> *The brightness of her cheek would shame those stars,*
> *As daylight doth a lamp; her eyes in heaven*
> *Would through the airy region stream so bright*
> *That birds would sing and think it were not night.*
> *See, how she leans her cheek upon her hand!*
> *O, that I were a glove upon that hand,*
> *That I might touch that cheek!*

Juliet

> *Aye me!*

He (*Mercutio*) makes fun of the pains he has never felt (*of being in love*).

But quiet! What light is coming through that window over there? It is east and Juliet is the sun! Rise up, beautiful sun and kill the jealous moon who is already sick and pale with grief over the fact that you are more beautiful than she. Do not subject yourself to her (*Juliet to the Moon i.e. Diana the goddess of virginity*), since she is jealous; her virgin's clothing (*moonlight*) is just pale and none but fools wear it; cast it off. It is my lady, oh, it is my love! Oh if only she knew it! She's speaking but not saying anything: how about that? Her eyes speak for her, I will answer them. I am too bold, it isn't to me she speaks: two of the fairest stars in all heaven, having some business have used her eyes to twinkle in their orbit until they return. What if her eyes were there, they (*the stars*) in her head? The brightness of her cheek could shame those stars, as daylight does the lamp. Her eyes would stream through the heavens so bright that birds would sing and think it was not night. See, how she leans her cheek upon her hand! Oh, that I were a glove upon that hand that I might touch that cheek!

(*Aye : Arrgghhh!*)

Romeo

> *She speaks: O, speak again, bright angel! for thou art*
> *As glorious to this night, being o'er my head*
> *As is a winged messenger of heaven*
> *Unto the white-upturned wondering eyes*
> *Of mortals that fall back to gaze on him*
> *When he bestrides the lazy-pacing clouds*
> *And sails upon the bosom of the air.*

She speaks! O, speak again bright angel! For you are as glorious to this night, being over my head, as is the winged messenger of heaven to the white, upturned wondering eyes (*because if you look up to the sky you expose the whites of your eyes*) of mortals that fall back to watch him as he strides the slow-moving clouds and sails upon the bosom of the air.

Juliet

> *O Romeo, Romeo! wherefore art thou Romeo?*
> *Deny thy father and refuse thy name;*
> *Or, if thou wilt not, be but sworn my love,*
> *And I'll no longer be a Capulet.*

O, Romeo, Romeo! Why do you have to be Romeo? Deny your father and refuse his name; Or, if you won't, be sworn my love and I'll no longer be a Capulet.

Romeo [Aside]

> *Shall I hear more or shall I speak at this?*

Juliet

> *'Tis but thy name that is my enemy;*
> *Thou art thyself, though not a Montague.*
> *What's Montague? it is nor hand, nor foot,*
> *Nor arm, nor face, nor any other part*

It's only your name that is my enemy; you are yourself, but not a Montague. What's Montague? It is not hand or foot or arm or face or any other part

28

Belonging to a man. O, be some other name!
What's in a name? that which we call a rose
By any other name would smell as sweet;
So Romeo would, were he not Romeo call'd,
Retain that dear perfection which he owns
Without that title. Romeo, doff thy name,
And for that name which is no part of thee
Take all myself.

Romeo

        I take thee at thy word:
Call me but love, and I'll be new baptized;
Henceforth I never will be Romeo.

Juliet

    What man art thou that thus bescreen'd in night
So stumblest on my counsel?

Romeo

    By a name I know not how to tell thee who I am:
My name, dear saint, is hateful to myself,
Because it is an enemy to thee;
Had I it written, I would tear the word.

Juliet

    My ears have not yet drunk a hundred words
Of that tongue's utterance, yet I know the sound:
Art thou not Romeo and a Montague?

Romeo

    Neither, fair saint, if either thee dislike.

Juliet

    How camest thou hither, tell me, and wherefore?
The orchard walls are high and hard to climb,
And the place death, considering who thou art,
If any of my kinsmen find thee here.

Romeo

    With love's light wings did I o'er-perch these walls;
For stony limits cannot hold love out,
And what love can do that dares love attempt;
Therefore thy kinsmen are no let to me.

Juliet

    If they do see thee, they will murder thee.

Romeo

    Alack, there lies more peril in thine eye
Than twenty of their swords: look thou but sweet,
And I am proof against their enmity.

Juliet

    I would not for the world they saw thee here.

Romeo

    I have night's cloak to hide me from their sight;
And but thou love me, let them find me here:
My life were better ended by their hate,
Than death prorogued, wanting of thy love.

Juliet

    By whose direction found'st thou out this place?

---

belonging to a man. Oh, be some other name!
What's in a name? That which we call a rose by
any other name would smell as sweet; so Romeo
would were he not Romeo called, keeping that
dear perfection which he owns without that title.
Romeo, lose your name and to replace that
name take all myself.

I take you at your word: call me your love and I'll
be new baptised; from now on I will never be
Romeo.

What man are you that hidden in the night
stumble on my private thoughts?

By a name I know not how to tell you who I am:
my name, dear saint, is hateful to myself
because it is an enemy to you; if I had it written I
would tear the word.

My ears have not drunk a hundred words of that
tongue's noises but I know the sound: are you
not Romeo and a Montague?

How came you here, tell me, and why? The
orchard walls are high and hard to climb and the
place is death, considering who you are, if any of
my [kinsmen : family] find you here.

With love's light wings did I climb over these
walls; for stone boundaries cannot hold love out
and what love can do, love dares to attempt;
therefore your kinsmen are no threat to me.

If they do see you they will murder you.

Alas, there's more peril [danger] in your eye than
twenty of their swords: all you have to do is look
sweet and I will be protected from their hate.

I would not for the world they saw you here.

I have night's cloak to hide me from their sight;
And if you love me, let them find me here: my life
were better ended by their hate than death
prolonged by wanting your love.

Who gave you directions to this place?

Romeo

> By love, who first did prompt me to inquire;
> He lent me counsel and I lent him eyes.
> I am no pilot; yet, wert thou as far
> As that vast shore wash'd with the farthest sea,
> I would adventure for such merchandise.

Juliet

> Thou know'st the mask of night is on my face,
> Else would a maiden blush bepaint my cheek
> For that which thou hast heard me speak to-night
> Fain would I dwell on form, fain, fain deny
> What I have spoke: but farewell compliment!
> Dost thou love me? I know thou wilt say 'Ay,'
> And I will take thy word: yet if thou swear'st,
> Thou mayst prove false; at lovers' perjuries
> Then say, Jove laughs. O gentle Romeo,
> If thou dost love, pronounce it faithfully:
> Or if thou think'st I am too quickly won,
> I'll frown and be perverse an say thee nay,
> So thou wilt woo; but else, not for the world.
> In truth, fair Montague, I am too fond,
> And therefore thou mayst think my 'havior light:
> But trust me, gentleman, I'll prove more true
> Than those that have more cunning to be strange.
> I should have been more strange, I must confess,
> But that thou overheard'st, ere I was ware,
> My true love's passion: therefore pardon me,
> And not impute this yielding to light love,
> Which the dark night hath so discovered.

Romeo

> Lady, by yonder blessed moon I swear
> That tips with silver all these fruit-tree tops-

Juliet

> O, swear not by the moon, the inconstant moon,
> That monthly changes in her circled orb,
> Lest that thy love prove likewise variable.

Romeo

> What shall I swear by?

Juliet

> Do not swear at all;
> Or, if thou wilt, swear by thy gracious self,
> Which is the god of my idolatry and I'll believe thee.

Romeo

> If my heart's dear love-

Juliet

> Well, do not swear: although I joy in thee,
> I have no joy of this contract to-night:
> It is too rash, too unadvised, too sudden;
> Too like the lightning, which doth cease to be
> Ere one can say 'It lightens.' Sweet, good night!
> This bud of love, by summer's ripening breath,

Love did, who first did prompt me to ask; he gave me advice and I gave him eyes. I am no pilot [*pilots originally steered ships not planes*] yet even if you were as far away as that huge shore washed by the furthest sea [*America*], I would adventure there for such a booty.

You know the mask of night is on my face, otherwise a maiden's blushing would paint my cheeks because of what you have heard me speak tonight. Gladly I would think about my appearance, gladly, gladly deny what I have spoken but [it's too late now so] farewell courtesy [*she is saying she would like to flirt but now the jig is up*]! Do you love me? I know you will say 'yes' and I will take you at your word: but if you swear it then you might prove false, as they say God [*Jove : Jupiter : Zeus*] laughs when men tell lies to seduce women. Oh gentle Romeo, if you do love me say it truly: or if you think I am too quickly won, I'll frown and be perverse and tell you no so you will flirt but anything else [than your love] I do not want for all the world. In truth, fair Montague, I am too fond and therefore you may think my behaviour a laughing matter. But trust me, gentleman, I'll prove more true [*as a wife*] than those that have the cunning to be strange. I should have been more standoffish, I must confess, but because you overheard me before I was aware of you, [*talking about*] my true love's passion [there's no point]. Therefore excuse me and do not consider this giving in to be thin love which this dark night has discovered.

Lady, by that blessed moon that tips with silver all these fruit-trees-

-Oh, don't swear by the moon, the inconstant moon, that changes monthly in her circling orbit, in case your love should prove likewise.

Do not swear at all or if you do, swear by your gracious self which is the god I worship and I'll believe you.

Actually, do not swear: although it gives me joy to hear you do it, I have no joy of this contract tonight. It is too rash, too ill-advised, too sudden, too like the lightning which does cease to be before you can say 'it lightens'. Sweet, good night! This bud of love, by summer's ripening breath,

May prove a beauteous flower when next we meet.
Good night, good night! as sweet repose and rest
Come to thy heart as that within my breast!

may become a beautiful flower when we next meet. Good night, good night! As sweet peace of mind and rest come to your heart as that within my breast!

Romeo
      O, wilt thou leave me so unsatisfied?
Juliet
      What satisfaction canst thou have tonight?
Romeo
      The exchange of thy love's faithful vow for mine.
Juliet
      I gave thee mine before thou didst request it:
And yet I would it were to give again.

I gave it to you before you had requested it: but I still wish I could give it to you again.

Romeo
   Wouldst thou withdraw it? for what purpose, love?

Would you take it away? For what purpose, love?

Juliet
      But to be frank, and give it thee again.
And yet I wish but for the thing I have:
My bounty is as boundless as the sea,
My love as deep; the more I give to thee,
The more I have, for both are infinite.

Just so I could be honest and give it to you again. And yet I wish only for the thing I already have: my treasure is as limitless as the sea, my love as deep. The more I give you the more I have, for both are infinite.

                              [Nurse calls within]
I hear some noise within; dear love, adieu!
Anon, good nurse! Sweet Montague, be true.
Stay but a little, I will come again.

I hear a noise within; dear love, goodbye! One minute good nurse! Sweet Montague, be true. Stay a moment and I will come again.

                              [Juliet exits, above]

Romeo
      O blessed, blessed night! I am afeard.
Being in night, all this is but a dream,
Too flattering-sweet to be substantial.

Oh blessed, blessed night! I am afraid, it being night, all this is but a dream, too flattering and sweet to be real.

            Enter Juliet, above
Juliet
      Three words, dear Romeo, and good night indeed.
If that thy bent of love be honourable,
Thy purpose marriage, send me word to-morrow,
By one that I'll procure to come to thee,
Where and what time thou wilt perform the rite;
And all my fortunes at thy foot I'll lay
And follow thee my lord throughout the world.
Nurse [Within]
            Madam!

Three words (*can you guess what they are??*) and good night indeed! If your romantic intentions be honourable, i.e. your purpose is marriage, send me word tomorrow by someone that I can send back to tell you where and what time we will perform the ceremony. And all my fortunes at your foot I'll lay and follow you my lord throughout the world.

Juliet
      I come, anon. - But if thou mean'st not well,
I do beseech thee -
Nurse [Within]
            Madam!

I'm coming, shortly – but if you don't mean well, I beg you -

Juliet
            By and by, I come!
- To cease thy suit, and leave me to my grief:
To-morrow will I send.

One minute, I'm coming! -To stop your games and leave me to my grief. Tomorrow I will send you a message.

31

Romeo

> So thrive my soul!

So prosper my soul!

Juliet

> A thousand times good night!

> > [Exit Juliet, above]

Romeo

> A thousand times the worse, to want thy light.
> Love goes toward love, as schoolboys from their books,
> But love from love, toward school with heavy looks.

A thousand times the harder I will crave your light. Love goes toward love as schoolboys go away from their books but love goes away from love as schoolboys go to school with heavy looks.

> > Romeo retires slowly.
> > Enter Juliet, above

Juliet

> Hist! Romeo, hist! O, for a falconer's voice,
> To lure this tassel-gentle back again!
> Bondage is hoarse, and may not speak aloud;
> Else would I tear the cave where Echo lies,
> And make her airy tongue more hoarse than mine,
> With repetition of my Romeo's name.

Pschh! Romeo, over here! Oh, for a falconer's voice to lure this [*tassel-gentle : a male hawk*] back again! Being restrained makes the voice hoarse and it may not speak aloud; otherwise I would tear open the cave where Echo [*a personification of echo*] lives and make her airy tongue more hoarse than mine with repetition of my Romeo's name.

Romeo

> It is my soul that calls upon my name:
> How silver-sweet sound lovers' tongues by night,
> Like softest music to attending ears!

It is my soul [*Juliet*] that calls upon my name: how silver-sweet sounding lover's tongues are by night like the softest music to listening ears!

Juliet

> Romeo!

Romeo

> My dear?

Juliet

> At what o'clock tomorrow shall I send to thee?

Romeo

> At the hour of nine.

Juliet

> I will not fail: 'tis twenty years till then.
> I have forgot why I did call thee back.

Romeo

> Let me stand here till thou remember it.

Juliet

> I shall forget, to have thee still stand there,
> Remembering how I love thy company.

Romeo

> And I'll still stay, to have thee still forget,
> Forgetting any other home but this.

In that case I'll definitely stay so that you still can't remember as I cannot imagine any other place I want to be than here like this.

Juliet

> 'Tis almost morning; I would have thee gone:
> And yet no further than a wanton's bird;
> Who lets it hop a little from her hand,
> Like a poor prisoner in his twisted gyves,
> And with a silk thread plucks it back again,
> So loving-jealous of his liberty.

It's almost the morning; I want you to go and yet no further than a spoilt child's bird that she lets hop in her hand like a poor prisoner in his twisted shackles and with a silk thread plucks it back again, so loving yet jealous of his freedom [*because birds can fly*].

Romeo

I would I were thy bird.

I wish I was this bird of yours.

Juliet

Sweet, so would I: Yet I should kill thee with much cherishing. Good night, good night! parting is such sweet sorrow, that I shall say good night till it be morrow.

Sweet, so would I: yet I would kill you with too much loving. Good night, good night! Parting in such sweet sorrow, that I will be saying good night until it is tomorrow.

[Exit Juliet, above]

Romeo

Sleep dwell upon thine eyes, peace in thy breast!
Would I were sleep and peace, so sweet to rest!
Hence will I to my ghostly friar's cell,
His help to crave, and my dear hap to tell.

Exit

Sleep dwell upon those eyes, peace in her breast! I wish I were sleep and peace, to help her rest! Now, I will go to my ghostly (*ghostly in the sense of spiritual*) friar (*Friar Lawrence, another character we are about to meet*)'s cell, his help to crave and my good fortune to tell.

II.III

A monk : A holy man who lives in a monastery.
A friar : A holy man who lives among the people.
Friar Laurence is a herbologist and he is a
certified magus when it comes to plants...

Friar Laurence's cell.
Enter Friar Laurence w basket

Friar Laurence

The grey-eyed morn smiles on the frowning night,
Chequering the eastern clouds with streaks of light,
And flecked darkness like a drunkard reels
From forth day's path and Titan's fiery wheels:
Now, ere the sun advance his burning eye,
The day to cheer and night's dank dew to dry,
I must up-fill this osier cage of ours
With baleful weeds and precious-juiced flowers.
The earth that's nature's mother is her tomb;
What is her burying grave that is her womb,
And from her womb children of divers kind
We sucking on her natural bosom find,
Many for many virtues excellent,
None but for some and yet all different.
O, mickle is the powerful grace that lies
In herbs, plants, stones, and their true qualities:
For nought so vile that on the earth doth live
But to the earth some special good doth give,
Nor aught so good but strain'd from that fair use
Revolts from true birth, stumbling on abuse:
Virtue itself turns vice, being misapplied;
And vice sometimes by action dignified.
Within the infant rind of this small flower
Poison hath residence and medicine power:
For this, being smelt, with that part cheers each part;
Being tasted, slays all senses with the heart.
Two such opposed kings encamp them still
In man as well as herbs, grace and rude will;
And where the worser is predominant,
Full soon the canker death eats up that plant.

Enter Romeo

Romeo

Good morrow, father.

Friar Laurence

Benedicite! What early tongue so sweet saluteth me?
Young son, it argues a distemper'd head
So soon to bid good morrow to thy bed:
Care keeps his watch in every old man's eye,
And where care lodges, sleep will never lie;
But where unbruised youth with unstuff'd brain
Doth couch his limbs, there golden sleep doth reign:
Therefore thy earliness doth me assure
Thou art up-roused by some distemperature;
Or if not so, then here I hit it right,
Our Romeo hath not been in bed tonight.

Romeo

That last is true; the sweeter rest was mine.

The grey-eyed morning smiles on the frowning night, colouring the eastern clouds with streaks of light and freckled darkness like a drunkard reels away from day's path and Titan's [*Helios the sun god rides a chariot that pulls the sun*] fiery wheels: now, before the sun advances [*over the sky*] his burning eye to cheer up the day and to dry night's damp dew, I must fill up this willow basket of ours with menacing weeds and precious-juice-filled flowers. The earth that is nature's mother is also her tomb; and her tomb that is the grave is also her womb and from her womb children [*plants*] of various kinds we find sucking on her natural bosom [*extracting water & nourishment from the earth*] and many of these children have many excellent virtues, except only a few who have none at all and yet all are different. Oh, [*mickle : great, the word has evolved into 'much'*] great is the powerful grace that lies in herbs, plants, stones and their true qualities: for none are so vile, of all those that live on the earth, that to the earth they cannot give some special goodness and neither are any so good that you could not stray from that fair use, revolting from it's true path and stumbling into abuse: Virtue itself turns into vice when misapplied and vice sometimes by action becomes dignified. Within the young skin of this small flower poison lives as well as medicine power: for this, being smelt by the nose cheers up the whole body; being tasted, slays all senses by stopping the heart. Two such rival kings encamp [*armies set up camps on battlefields*] in man as well as herbs, called grace and rude will; and where the worser is predominant, very soon the [*canker : cankerworm : an aggressive sort of caterpillar*] called death eats up that plant.

Good morning, father.

St. Benedict [*like saying, 'good lord'*]! What early morning tongue greets me so happy? Young son, it argues a disturbed mind to say goodnight to your bed, so early in the day. Care keeps his watch in every old man's eye and where care lodges, sleep will never lie; but where unbruised youth with an unstuffed brain does rest his limbs, there golden sleep reigns. Therefore, your earliness does assure me that you are worked-up by some 'dis-temperature' [*anxiety/illness*] or if not that, then here I get it right: our Romeo has not been in bed [at all] tonight.

The last thing you said is true; I enjoyed a sweeter rest [than sleep].

Friar Laurence
> God pardon sin! wast thou with Rosaline?

Romeo
> With Rosaline, my ghostly father?
> No; I have forgot that name and that name's woe.

Friar Laurence
> That's my good son: but where hast thou been, then?

Romeo
> I'll tell thee, ere thou ask it me again.
> I have been feasting with mine enemy,
> Where on a sudden one hath wounded me,
> That's by me wounded: both our remedies
> Within thy help and holy physic lies:
> I bear no hatred, blessed man, for, lo,
> My intercession likewise steads my foe.

Friar Laurence
> Be plain, good son, and homely in thy drift;
> Riddling confession finds but riddling shrift.

Romeo
> Then plainly know my heart's dear love is set
> On the fair daughter of rich Capulet:
> As mine on hers, so hers is set on mine;
> And all combined, save what thou must combine
> By holy marriage: when and where and how
> We met, we woo'd and made exchange of vow,
> I'll tell thee as we pass; but this I pray,
> That thou consent to marry us to-day.

Friar Laurence
> Holy Saint Francis, what a change is here!
> Is Rosaline, whom thou didst love so dear,
> So soon forsaken? young men's love then lies
> Not truly in their hearts, but in their eyes.
> Jesu Maria, what a deal of brine
> Hath wash'd thy sallow cheeks for Rosaline!
> How much salt water thrown away in waste,
> To season love, that of it doth not taste!
> The sun not yet thy sighs from heaven clears,
> Thy old groans ring yet in my ancient ears;
> Lo, here upon thy cheek the stain doth sit
> Of an old tear that is not wash'd off yet:
> If e'er thou wast thyself and these woes thine,
> Thou and these woes were all for Rosaline:
> And art thou changed? Pronounce this sentence then,
> Women may fall, when there's no strength in men.

Romeo
> Thou chid'st me oft for loving Rosaline.

Friar Laurence
> For doting, not for loving, pupil mine.

Romeo
> And bad'st me bury love.

Friar Laurence
> Not in a grave, to lay one in, another out to have.

[The Friar thinks Romeo means he was making love all night]

With Rosaline, my [*ghostly father : father of spirits*]? No; I have forgotten that name and that name's grief.

I'll tell you, before you ask it me again. I have been feasting with my enemy, where, on a sudden one, I was wounded by the one that is by me wounded: both our problems can be solved with your help and with your holy medicine: I bear no hatred, blessed man, for look, my asking you for help likewise helps my foe.

Be straight, good son and simple in your explanation; a riddle like confession will only result in a riddle like absolution.

Then plainly know my heart's dear love is set on the fair daughter of rich Capulet: as mine on hers, so hers is set on mine and we are all combined, except what you must combine by holy marriage. When and where and how we met, we wooed and made exchange of vow, I'll tell you as we go but this I pray: that you consent to marry us today.

Holy Saint Francis, what a change is here! Is Rosaline, who did love so dearly, so quickly forsaken? Young men's love then lies not truly in their hearts but in their eyes. Jesus and Mary, what a load of salt-water has washed your pale cheeks for Rosaline! How much salt water thrown away in waste to season [*as though cooking*] love that was never actually tasted! The sun hasn't finished clearing your sighs from heaven, your old groans still ring in my ancient ears; look, here upon your cheek the stain still sits of an old tear that is not washed off yet: if ever you were yourself and those woes yours, you and those woes were all for Rosaline, then have you really changed so much? Repeat this sentence then: women may fall when there's no strength in men.

You cussed me often for loving Rosaline.

For obsessing, not for loving, my pupil.

And commanded me to bury [that] love.

Not in a grave, to lay one in while you take up another.

Romeo

    I pray thee, chide not; she whom I love now
Doth grace for grace and love for love allow;
The other did not so.

Friar Laurence

        O, she knew well
Thy love did read by rote and could not spell.
But come, young waverer, come, go with me,
In one respect I'll thy assistant be;
For this alliance may so happy prove,
To turn your households' rancour to pure love.

Romeo

    O, let us hence; I stand on sudden haste.

Friar Laurence

    Wisely and slow; they stumble that run fast.

               Exeunt

I beg you, don't get mad at me: she who I love now does return my grace and love, the other did not so.

Oh, she knew well your love did read by repetition and could not spell (*as though he was illiterate and learnt to pretend how to spell; as though he was ignorant of true virtue and only knew how to pretend to love*). But come, young wanderer, come, go with me, in one respect I'll your assistant be; for this alliance may prove to be so happy that it could turn your household's rivalry into pure love.

O, mickle is the powerful grace that lies
In herbs, plants, stones, and their true qualities:
For nought so vile that on the earth doth live
But to the earth some special good doth give,
Nor aught so good but strain'd from that fair use
Revolts from true birth, stumbling on abuse

II.IV

Verona's streets.
Enter Benvolio & Mercutio

Mercutio
Where the devil should this Romeo be?
-Came he not home tonight?

Where the hell is Romeo? Didn't come home last night?

Benvolio
Not to his father's; I spoke with his man.

Not to his father's, I spoke with his old man.

Mercutio
Ah, that same pale hard-hearted wench, that Rosaline
Torments him so, that he will sure run mad.

Ah, that same pale hard-hearted b * * * Rosaline torments him so much that he will surely turn mad.

Benvolio
Tybalt, the kinsman of old Capulet,
  Hath sent a letter to his father's house.

Tybalt, a home-boy of old Capulet, has sent a message to his father's house.

Mercutio
A challenge, on my life.

He wants me to fight him to the death!?

Benvolio
Romeo will answer it.

(*Romeo will duel with him*)

Mercutio
Any man that can write may answer a letter.

Benvolio
Nay, he will answer the letter's master,
  how he dares, being dared.

No, he must answer the letter's sender with a reply whether he dares fight or not, after being challenged (*Romeo must stand up for himself*).

Mercutio
Alas poor Romeo! he is already dead; stabbed
with a white wench's black eye; shot through the ear
with a love-song; the very pin of his heart cleft with
the blind bow-boy's butt-shaft: and is he a man to
encounter Tybalt?

Oh dear, poor Romeo! He is already dead – stabbed by a white chick's [beautiful] dark eyes; shot through the ear with a love-song; cut right through the middle of his heart with a young blind archer's practise arrow: do you think he's capable of taking on Tybalt?

Benvolio
Why, what is Tybalt?

Mercutio
More than prince of cats, I can tell you.
O, he is the courageous captain of compliments.
He fights as you sing prick-song, keeps time, distance,
and proportion; rests me his minim rest, one, two,
and the third in your bosom: the very butcher of a silk
button, a duellist, a duellist; a gentleman of the
very first house, of the first and second cause:
ah, the immortal passado! The punto reverso!
  The hay!

(*Reference to 'Tibault, Prince of Cats', an old Dutch fable:*) More than the Prince of Cats, I can tell you. Oh, he is the master of ceremonies. He fights by the book (*prick-song : printed music*), keeping good timing, distance and rhythm; pauses like the brief rests in music, one, two and the then on third [sticks his sword] in your chest: he's so damn good that he can cut the silk button from your shirt, a duellist, a duellist; a gentleman of the very best school of fencing, of the first and second strike (*the correct conditions for a proper gent to duel*) ah, the forward thrust, that never gets old! The backhanded thrust! The hay-maker!

Benvolio
The what?

(*Benvolio isn't familiar with the term 'hay'*)

Mercutio
The pox of such antic, lisping, affecting
fantasticoes; these new tuners of accents! 'By Jesu,
a very good blade! a very tall man! a very good
whore!' Why, is not this a lamentable thing,
grandsire, that we should be thus afflicted with

The ('*all this fancy posh slang '...*) vain stupidity of antique, lisping, over-the-top fantastical language; the new tuners of accents! 'By Jesus, a very a good blade! A very brave man! A very good whore!' Why, isn't it such a shame, grandpa, that we should be under-siege from these strange

37

these strange flies, these fashion-mongers, these
pardon-moi's, who stand so much on the new form,
that they cannot at ease on the old bench?
                    O, their bones, their bones!

crazes, these fashion-mongers, these
'excuse-me's who are so keen on their new
school that they cannot do the old school? Oh,
[curse] their bones, [curse] their bones!!

Enter Romeo

Benvolio
        Here comes Romeo, here comes Romeo.
Mercutio
        Without his roe, like a dried herring: flesh,
flesh, how art thou fishified! Now is he for the
numbers that Petrarch flowed in: Laura to his lady
was but a kitchen-wench; marry, she had a better love
to be-rhyme her; Dido a dowdy; Cleopatra a gipsy;
Helen and Hero hildings and harlots; Thisbe a grey
eye or so, but not to the purpose. Signior
Romeo, bon jour! there's a French salutation
to your French slop. You gave us the counterfeit
fairly last night.

Like a fish that has laid it's eggs (*much thinner*),
like a dried herring: flesh, flesh how you are
fishified! Now he's trying to go on like (*Petrarch:
Italian love poet obsessed with a girl called
Laura*): Laura was just a kitchen-girl; mind you,
she had a better lover writing poems to her
(*Petrarch is better poet than Romeo*). Dido
(*Aeneas' fling*) was a bit shabby, Cleopatra (*of
Egypt*) was a gipsy, Helen (*of Troy*) and Hero (*a
character from Shakespeare's rival Marlowe*)
were good-for-nothing tarts; Thisbe (*from Ovid's
Metamorphosis as depicted in A Midsummer
Night's Dream*) had grey eyes (*which were
considered to be very beautiful in Shakespeare's
day*) but isn't worth mentioning. Signior Romeo,
bon jour! There's a French salutation for your
French garms (*Romeo is still wearing his party
clothes*)! You gave us the 'counterfeit' very well
last night.

Romeo
        Good morrow to you both.
                    What counterfeit did I give you?

Good morning to you both! What did I show you
last night?

Mercutio
        The slip, sir, the slip; can you not conceive?

(*Counterfeit coins were nick-named 'slips'*); don't
you get it?

Romeo
        Pardon, good Mercutio, my business was
great; and in such a case as mine a man may strain
courtesy.

Excuse me, good Mercutio, my business was
great and in such a case as mine a man might
have to put good manners to the side for one
moment.

Mercutio
        That's as much as to say, such a case as yours
constrains a man to bow in the hams.

That's about as good as saying such a case as
yours restrains you from bowing from the waist
(*as he should because he has been rude to his
friends / he cannot do so because he has a
painful S.T.D.*)

Romeo
        Meaning, to court'sy.

By which you mean to give a little nod [as that is
all you deserve].

Mercutio
        Thou hast most kindly hit it.

You've hit the nail on the head.

Romeo
        A most courteous exposition.

You gave me a polite and courteous explanation.

Mercutio
        Nay, I am the very pink of courtesy.

Nay, I am the very colour of courtesy.

Romeo
        Pink for flower.

Pink like a flower?!

Mercutio
        Right.

Romeo

Why, then is my pump well flowered.

Mercutio

Well said: follow me this jest now till thou hast worn out thy pump, that when the single sole of it is worn, the jest may remain after the wearing sole singular.

Romeo

O single-soled jest, solely singular for the singleness.

Mercutio

Come between us, good Benvolio; my wits faint.

Romeo

Switch and spurs, switch and spurs; or I'll cry a match.

Mercutio

Nay, if thy wits run the wild-goose chase, I have done, for thou hast more of the wild-goose in one of thy wits than, I am sure, I have in my whole five: was I with you there for the goose?

Romeo

Thou wast never with me for any thing when thou wast not there for the goose.

Mercutio

I will bite thee by the ear for that jest.

Romeo

Nay, good goose, bite not.

Mercutio

Thy wit is a very bitter sweeting;
　　　　　　　it is a most sharp sauce.

Romeo

And is it not well served in to a sweet goose?

Mercutio

O here's a wit of cheveril, that stretches from an inch narrow to an ell broad!

Romeo

I stretch it out for that word 'broad;' which added to the goose, proves thee far and wide a broad goose.

Mercutio

Why, is not this better now than groaning for love? Now art thou sociable, now art thou Romeo; now art thou what thou art, by art as well as by nature: for this drivelling love is like a great natural, that runs lolling up and down to hide his bauble in a hole.

Benvolio

Stop there, stop there!

Mercutio

Thou desirest me to stop in my tale against the hair.

Benvolio

Thou wouldst else have made thy tale large.

Why, then my shoe is well flowered (*my party shoes are very 'courteous' because they have pink ribbons on them*).

Well said: follow me with these jokes until you have worn out your shoe, so that when the soles are worn out, the jokes will remain behind after the wearing of those shoes is finished it's one lifetime.

Oh what a thin-witted joke, that is only different for the sake of being original.

Break us up, good Benvolio, I can't do this any more.

Use whips and spurs, whips and spurs (*to keep yourself going*) or I'll cry game, set, match!

No, if your game is a wild-goose chase then I am finished, for you have more of the wild-goose in one of your wits than I have in my whole five (*Shakespeare's 5 wits*). Was I with you there, behaving like a goose (*looking for a prostitute*)?

You was never with me for any thing when there was not a prostitute involved.

I will bite off your ear for that joke.

Your wit is a very bitter apple-sauce; it is a most sharp sauce.

And is it not well served with (*roast*) goose?

Oh here's a wit of (*cheveril : stretchy leather*) that stretches from an inch narrow to 45 inches broad!

I stretch it out so that it will fit that word 'broad', which added to the goose proves you are far and widely regarded as a big goose.

Why, is not this better now than groaning for love? Now you are sociable, now you are Romeo; now are you what you are, in manner as well as in nature; for this drivelling love is like a great idiot that runs up and down with his tongue hanging out, trying to hide his (*bauble : the stick a court jester carries, like the ones a joker holds in a deck of cards*) in a hole (*sexual innuendo*).

Hold up, hold up!

You want me to stop in my tale against the grain (*'just when it was getting good'*).

You would have made your tale large.

Mercutio

O, thou art deceived; I would have made it short: for I was come to the whole depth of my tale; and meant, indeed, to occupy the argument no longer.

Oh, you are deceived; I would have made it short: for I come to the whole thrust of my tale[/tail] and didn't mean to spend any more time on the matter.

Romeo

Here's goodly gear!

Here's some good stuff!

Enter Nurse & Peter

Mercutio

A sail, a sail!

('something of interest is coming to shore!')

Benvolio

Two, two; a shirt and a smock.

Two, two (sails); a shirt and a gown (a man and a woman).

Nurse

Peter!

Peter

Anon!

One second [I'm coming]!

Nurse

My fan, Peter.

(to cool off with; Peter is Nurses' chaperone)

Mercutio

Good Peter, to hide her face;
for her fan's the fairer face.

Good Peter, give it to her to hide her face, for the fan looks much nicer.

Nurse

God ye good morrow, gentlemen.

God give you a good morning, gentlemen.

Mercutio

God ye good den, fair gentlewoman.

God give you a good afternoon, gentlewoman.

Nurse

Is it good den?

Is it afternoon [already]?

Mercutio

'Tis no less, I tell you, for the bawdy hand of the dial is now upon the prick of noon.

It is no less, I tell you, for the lewd hand of the dial (dial: slang for face) is now upon the prick of noon (yes, he is that rude).

Nurse

Out upon you! what a man are you!

Be gone with you! What kind of man are you?!

Romeo

One, gentlewoman, that God hath made for himself to mar.

One, gentlewoman, that God has made for himself to look imperfect.

Nurse

By my troth, it is well said; 'for himself to mar,' quoth'a? Gentlemen, can any of you tell me where I may find the young Romeo?

By my faith, it is well said 'for himself to scar' he says? Gentlemen, can any of you tell me where I may find the young Romeo?

Romeo

I can tell you; but young Romeo will be older when you have found him than he was when you sought him: I am the youngest of that name, for fault of a worse.

I can tell you but young Romeo will be older when you have found him than he was when you sought him. I am the youngest of that name for lack of a worse one (normally, 'better one').

Nurse

You say well.

I like your style.

Mercutio

Yea, is the worst well? Very well took, i' faith; wisely, wisely.

Indeed, is the worst well? Very well understood, in faith, wisely, wisely (he is making fun of her for thinking Romeo was humble when in fact Romeo was speaking well of himself)

Nurse

    If you be he, sir, I desire some confidence with you.

If you are him, sir, I would like to talk in private.

Benvolio

    She will indite him to some supper.

She will (*indite : he uses the wrong word, instead of invite, because he is making fun of her not being able to keep up with their banter*) him to some supper.

Mercutio

    A bawd, a bawd, a bawd! So ho!

(*A bawd! : a hunter's signal that he has seen a hare*)

Romeo

    What hast thou found?

What have you seen?!

Mercutio

    No hare, sir; unless a hare, sir, in a lenten pie, that is something stale and hoar ere it be spent.

No hare, sir, unless a hare, sir, in a (*lenten pie: pie made during lent i.e. without meat*) that is very stale and mouldy before it is eaten (*Mercutio is being rude about Nurse. Make of the poem what you will – but I warned you that Mercutio is completely nuts*).

        [Singing]
           An old hare hoar,
           And an old hare hoar,
           Is very good meat in lent
           But a hare that is hoar
           Is too much for a score,
           When it hoars ere it be spent.
        Romeo, will you come to your father's?
    We'll to dinner, thither.

Romeo, will you come to your father's? We're going to dinner there.

Romeo

    I will follow you.

Mercutio

    Farewell, ancient lady; farewell,
        [Singing]
    'lady, lady, lady.'
        [Exeunt Mercutio & Benvolio]

Nurse

    Marry, farewell! I pray you, sir, what saucy merchant was this, that was so full of his ropery?

My goodness, farewell ['and good riddance']! I pray you, sir, what saucy hustler was that, so full of tricks?

Romeo

    A gentleman, Nurse, that loves to hear himself talk, and will speak more in a minute than he will stand to in a month.

A gentleman, Nurse, that loves to hear himself talk and will speak more in a minute than he will make good on in a month.

Nurse

    An a' speak any thing against me, I'll take him down, an a' were lustier than he is, and twenty such Jacks; and if I cannot, I'll find those that shall. Scurvy knave! I am none of his flirt-gills; I am none of his skains-mates. And thou must stand by too, and suffer every knave to use me at his pleasure?

And if he says anything bad about me, I'll take him down even if he were more vigorous than he was just now, him plus twenty such Jacks and if I cannot, I'll find those that can. Scurvy knave! I am none of his promiscuous girlfriends, I am none of his dagger-buddies. And you (*Peter*) just standing there, letting every knave use me at his pleasure (*sexual innuendo*)?

Peter

    I saw no man use you a pleasure; if I had, my weapon should quickly have been out, I warrant you: I dare draw as soon as another man, if I see occasion in a good quarrel, and the law on my side.

I saw no man use you at his pleasure! If I had, my weapon should quickly have been out, I'm telling you: I'm as ready to engage as the next man, if I see a good reason to get it on and the law is on my side.

Nurse

Now, afore God, I am so vexed, that every part about me quivers. Scurvy knave! Pray you, sir, a word: and as I told you, my young lady bade me inquire you out; what she bade me say, I will keep to myself: but first let me tell ye, if ye should lead her into a fool's paradise, as they say, it were a very gross kind of behavior, as they say: for the gentlewoman is young; and, therefore, if you should deal double with her, truly it were an ill thing and very weak dealing.

Now, before God, I am so vexed that every part about me quivers. Scurvy knave! Pray you, sir, a word: and as I told you, my young lady asked me to find you out; what she told me to say, I will keep to myself but first let me tell you, if you should lead her into a 'fool's paradise' as they say, it were a very 'gross kind of behaviour', as they say: for the gentlewoman is young and therefore if you should deal-double with her, truly, it would be a bad thing and very weak dealing.

Romeo

Nurse, commend me to thy lady and mistress. I protest unto thee!

Nurse, tell your lady and mistress that I am good. I demand of you!

Nurse

Good heart, and, i' faith, I will tell her as much: Lord, Lord, she will be a joyful woman.

Good heart and in faith, I will tell her as much: Lord, Lord, she will be a joyful woman.

Romeo

What wilt thou tell her, Nurse? Thou dost not mark me.

What will you tell her, Nurse? You're not paying attention to me.

Nurse

I will tell her, sir, that you do protest; which, as I take it, is a gentlemanlike offer.

I will tell her, sir, that you do demand; which, as I take it, is a gentlemanly show [of affection].

Romeo

Bid her devise Some means to come to shrift this afternoon; and there she shall at Friar Laurence' cell be shrived and married. Here is for thy pains.

Get her to devise some way of coming to confession this afternoon; and there in Friar Laurence's cell she will be absolved and married. Here is for your troubles [*giving her money*]...

Nurse

No truly sir; not a penny.

Romeo

Go to; I say you shall.

Nurse

This afternoon, sir? well, she shall be there.

Romeo

And stay, good Nurse, behind the abbey wall: Within this hour my man shall be with thee And bring thee cords made like a tackled stair; Which to the high top-gallant of my joy Must be my convoy in the secret night. Farewell; be trusty, and I'll quit thy pains: Farewell; commend me to thy mistress.

And wait, good Nurse, behind the abbey wall: within this hour my friend will come to you and bring three cords made like a rope-ladder; which to the [*top-gallant: highest mast on a ship*] highest point of my joy must be my means of travel in the secret night *[he intends for her to take it back to the Capulet mansion as best for him to reach Juliet later at night*]. Farewell, be trusting and I'll pay you for your troubles. Farewell, commend me to your mistress.

Nurse

Now God in heaven bless thee! Hark you, sir.

[*Hark : listen closely*]

Romeo

What say'st thou, my dear Nurse?

Nurse

Is your man secret? Did you ne'er hear say, Two may keep counsel, putting one away?

Is your friend secretive? Did you never hear the saying [*Two may... : 1. two people can keep a secret if one of them dies i.e. two people can't keep a secret 3. two people can keep a secret if they are conspiring to affect a third person*].

42

Romeo

I warrant thee, my man's as true as steel.

Nurse

Well, sir; my mistress is the sweetest lady —
Lord, Lord! When 'twas a little prating thing.
O, there is a nobleman in town, one Paris, that would
fain lay knife aboard; but she, good soul, had as lief
see a toad, a very toad, as see him. I anger her
sometimes and tell her that Paris is the properer
man; but, I'll warrant you, when I say so, she looks
as pale as any clout in the versal world. Doth not
rosemary and Romeo begin both with a letter?

Romeo

Ay, Nurse; what of that? Both with an R.

Nurse

Ah. mocker! that's the dog's name; R is for
the - No; I know it begins with some other
letter - and she hath the prettiest sententious of
it, of you and rosemary, that it would do you good
to hear it.

Romeo

Commend me to thy lady.

Nurse

Ay, a thousand times.

                                        [Exit Romeo]
                    Peter!

Peter

Anon!

Nurse

Peter, take my fan, and go before and apace.
                                        Exeunt

Well sir, my mistress is the sweetest lady –
Lord, Lord! When she was a little chattering
thing – Oh, there is a nobleman in town, one
Paris, who is eager to lay claim [*in those days
one might choose their place at the dinner table
by putting their knife there*]: but she, good soul,
would as willingly date a toad, a very toad rather
than be seeing him. I anger her sometimes and
tell her that Paris is a proper man but I'll tell you,
when I say so, she looks as pale as any dishcloth
in all the world. Does not rosemary [*the herb of
remembrance & funerals*] and Romeo begin
both with the same letter [*the Nurse is illiterate
which explains her linguistic mistakes*]?

[*Ay : Yes*]

Ah, joker! That's the dog's name [*R was
associated with a dog's growl; 'grrrrr'*] ; R is for
the – no, I know it begins with some other
letter – and she says the prettiest things about
you and rosemary, you should hear her going on.

II.V

Capulet's Orchard.
Enter Juliet

Juliet

The clock struck nine when I did send the
Nurse; In half an hour she promised to return.
Perchance she cannot meet him: that's not so.
O, she is lame! love's heralds should be thoughts,
Which ten times faster glide than the sun's beams,
Driving back shadows over louring hills:
Therefore do nimble-pinion'd doves draw love,
And therefore hath the wind-swift Cupid wings.
Now is the sun upon the highmost hill
Of this day's journey, and from nine till twelve
Is three long hours, yet she is not come.
Had she affections and warm youthful blood,
She would be as swift in motion as a ball;
My words would bandy her to my sweet love,
And his to me: But old folks, many feign as they were
dead; Unwieldy, slow, heavy and pale as lead.
O God, she comes!

The clock struck nine when I sent the Nurse; In half an hour she promised to return. Maybe she cannot meet him – no, that can't be. Oh, she is lame! Love's messengers should be thoughts, which glide ten times faster than the sun's beams, driving back shadows over scowling hills: in this way light-winged doves draw love [*in mythology, doves drew Venus' chariot*] and so the wind-swift Cupid has wings. Now the sun has reached the highest hill of this day's journey and from nine until twelve is three long hours, yet she is not come. If she was as affectionate and warm as youthful blood she would be swift in motion as a tennis ball; my words would bounce her back and forth to my sweet love and his to me: but old folks, many act as though they were already dead; difficult to use, slow, heavy and pale as lead. O God, she comes!

Enter Nurse & Peter

O honey Nurse, what news?
Hast thou met with him? Send thy man away.

Nurse

Peter, stay at the gate.

[Exit Peter]

Juliet

Now, good sweet Nurse, O Lord, why look'st
thou sad? Though news be sad, yet tell them merrily;
If good, thou shamest the music of sweet news
By playing it to me with so sour a face.

Now, good sweet Nurse, oh Lord, why do you look so sad? Although news is sometimes sad you must tell it merrily; if good, you shame the music of sweet news by playing it to me with so sour a face.

Nurse

I am a-weary, give me leave awhile:
Fie, how my bones ache! what a jaunt have I had!

I am weary, give me break for a minute: [*fie : damn*] my bones are aching. What a journey I have had!

Juliet

I would thou hadst my bones, and I thy news:
Nay, come, I pray thee, speak; good, good Nurse,
speak.

I wish you had my bones and I your news: nay, come, I beg you, speak; good, good Nurse, speak.

Nurse

Jesu, what haste? Can you not stay awhile?
Do you not see that I am out of breath?

Jesus, why such a hurry? Can you not wait a minute? Do you not see I am out of breath?

Juliet

How art thou out of breath, when thou hast breath
To say to me that thou art out of breath?
The excuse that thou dost make in this delay
Is longer than the tale thou dost excuse.
Is thy news good, or bad? answer to that;
Say either, and I'll stay the circumstance:
Let me be satisfied, is't good or bad?

How are you out of breath, when you have enough breath to say to me that you are out of breath? The excuses that you make in this delay are longer than the tale that you do excuse. Is your news good or bad? Answer to that; say either and I can wait for the details: let me be satisfied, is it good or bad?

Nurse

Well, you have made a simple choice; you know
not how to choose a man: Romeo! no, not he; though
his face be better than any man's, yet his leg excels
all men's; and for a hand, and a foot, and a body,
though they be not to be talked on, yet they are
past compare: he is not the flower of courtesy,
but, I'll warrant him, as gentle as a lamb. Go thy
ways, wench; serve God. What, have you dined at
home?

Juliet

No, no: but all this did I know before.
What says he of our marriage? What of that?

Nurse

Lord, how my head aches! What a head have I!
It beats as it would fall in twenty pieces.
My back o' t' other side, O, my back, my back!
Beshrew your heart for sending me about,
To catch my death with jaunting up and down!

Juliet

I' faith, I am sorry that thou art not well. Sweet,
sweet, sweet Nurse, tell me, what says my love?

Nurse

Your love says, like an honest gentleman, and a
courteous, and a kind, and a handsome, and, I
warrant, a virtuous - where is your mother?

Juliet

Where is my mother! why, she is within;
Where should she be? How oddly thou repliest!
'Your love says, like an honest gentleman,
Where is your mother?'

Nurse

O God's lady dear! Are you so hot? marry,
come up, I trow; Is this the poultice for my aching
bones? Henceforward do your messages yourself.

Juliet

Here's such a coil! come, what says Romeo?

Nurse

Have you got leave to go to shrift to-day?

Juliet

I have.

Nurse

Then hie you hence to Friar Laurence's cell;
There stays a husband to make you a wife:
Now comes the wanton blood up in your cheeks,
They'll be in scarlet straight at any news.
Hie you to church; I must another way,
To fetch a ladder, by the which your love
Must climb a bird's nest soon when it is dark:
I am the drudge and toil in your delight,
But you shall bear the burden soon at night.

Well, you have made a simple choice; you don't
know how to choose a man: Romeo! No, not he,
even if his face is better than any man's, even if
his leg excels all men's, and for a hand and a foot
and a body even though they are past compare,
he is not the flower of courtesy but he is gentle
as a lamb, I'll give him that. Do whatever you
wish, (*wench : affectionate name 'little
troublemaker'*), and serve God. What, have you
had your dinner yet?

Where is my mother? Why she is within, where
else would she be? How oddly you reply; "Your
love says, like an honest gentleman, where is
your mother?".

Oh God's lady the dear Virgin Mary! Are you so
hot? Truly, you should calm down I think. Is this
the (*poultice : like the opposite of an ice-pack,
when you put warm moist bread on a wound*)
for my aching bones? From now on, you send
your messages yourself.

What a fuss! Come, what did Romeo say?

Have you got permission to go to confession
today?

Then off you go to Friar Laurence's cell; there is
waiting a husband to make you a wife. Now I see
the lustful blood up in your cheeks, they'll turn
scarlet red at any news. Get yourself to church; I
must go somewhere else to fetch a ladder by
which your love must climb to a bird's nest when
it is dark (*her bedroom*):I am the slave and work
in your delight but you will bear the burden (*1. as
in being a good wife for an entire lifetime*) soon
at night (*2. as in support the weight of the man
physically during intercourse*).

Go; I'll to dinner: hie you to the cell.

Go, I'm gonna get some dinner – hurry yourself to the cell [*Friar Laurence's residence*].

Juliet

Hie to high fortune! Honest Nurse, farewell.

Exeunt

II.VI

Friar Laurence's cell.
Enter Friar Laurence & Romeo

Friar Laurence

So smile the heavens upon this holy act,
That after hours with sorrow chide us not!

So let the heavens smile upon this holy act (*Romeo & Juliet's marriage*) that 'after-hours' [*in the coming days*] with sorrow doesn't put us down.

Romeo

Amen, amen! but come what sorrow can,
It cannot countervail the exchange of joy
That one short minute gives me in her sight:
Do thou but close our hands with holy words,
Then love-devouring death do what he dare;
It is enough I may but call her mine.

Amen, amen! But come what sorrow can, it cannot outweigh the exchange of joy that one short minute gives me in her sight. When you have closed our hands with holy words then love-devouring death, do what he dare, it is enough that I may call her mine.

Friar Laurence

These violent delights have violent ends
And in their triumph die, like fire and powder,
Which as they kiss consume: the sweetest honey
Is loathsome in his own deliciousness
And in the taste confounds the appetite:
Therefore love moderately; long love doth so;
Too swift arrives as tardy as too slow.

These violent delights have violent ends and in their triumph die like fire and gunpowder, which as they kiss consume [*ignite*] [each other]. The very sweetest of honey is a problem to it's own deliciousness and when tasted confuses the appetite; therefore, love moderately, long love does so; being too fast can be as unhelpful as being too slow.

Enter Juliet
Here comes the lady: O, so light a foot
Will ne'er wear out the everlasting flint:
A lover may bestride the gossamer
That idles in the wanton summer air,
And yet not fall; so light is vanity.

Here comes the lady – Oh, so light of foot would never wear out the hard-stoned cobbled pavement. A lover can walk along the threads of spider-webs that float through the luxurious summer air and not fall; so light is the brief joy experienced by human beings.

Juliet

Good even to my ghostly confessor.

Good evening my spiritual confessor.

Friar Laurence [*as Romeo kisses her passionately*]

Romeo shall thank thee, daughter, for us both.

Romeo shall thank you, daughter, for us both.

Juliet [*kissing him in return*]

As much to him, else is his thanks too much.

As many thanks to him too, or else he thanks too much.

Romeo

Ah, Juliet, if the measure of thy joy
Be heap'd like mine and that thy skill be more
To blazon it, then sweeten with thy breath
This neighbour air, and let rich music's tongue
Unfold the imagined happiness that both
Receive in either by this dear encounter.

Ah, Juliet, if the measure of your joy is heaped like mine and if your good-sense declares it then sweeten with your breath this air which we share and let rich music's language unfold the imagined happiness that both of us are going to get from the other because of this priceless encounter.

Juliet

Conceit, more rich in matter than in words,
Brags of his substance, not of ornament:
They are but beggars that can count their worth;
But my true love is grown to such excess
I cannot sum up sum of half my wealth.

This vain fantasy, more rich in matter than in words [*this is a matter of science more than opinion*] brags of what he is made of, not what he looks like: there are even beggars who think highly of themselves; but my true love is grown to such excess, I can't even count half my wealth.

Friar Laurence
> Come, come with me, and we will make short work;
> For, by your leaves, you shall not stay alone
> Till holy church incorporate two in one.
> *Exeunt*

Come, come with me and we'll make short work: for, with your permissions, you will not live on alone but holy church will make the two of you into one.

The real church of the real Verona. Photographed by **Lo Scaligero**

Commentary : Act II

We are now entering the phases of true love, of love that almost precipitates physically into the air, crackling with waves of energy that pulse back and forth along the circuits of lover's hearts. His hot-headed daring, spurring him on, getting him all worked up and in love. Her lack of 'strangeness', embarrassment and young sensuality. Their insatiable hunger to please each other.

It is astounding how flawlessly Shakespeare executes these sequences of thoughts and emotions between his characters; Juliet's embarrassment at having been overheard openly declaring her affection for Romeo (plus the fact she is very young and from what little we see of her life and as indeed would be normal given the cultural context she has barley seen anything of the world, therefore making Romeo's intrusion quite the trespass) results in this kind of sensible self-restraint that glosses over her involvement with modest maturity and brings the enterprise to whole new levels of sincerity. She forces Romeo to promise he is not 'leading her in a fools paradise,' as Nurse would say, openly confessing that she is unskilled in such practises and feels likely to be played for a fool if what she has heard is true: *"If though thinkest I am too quickly won, I'll frown and be perverse and say thee 'nay' so thou wilt woo,"* And then later on *"Swear not by the inconstant moon, that monthly changes in her circled orb, lest that thy love prove likewise variable,"* What is being demonstrated is a well known fact: by holding back a little we do in fact invigorate a relationship and increase the intensity threefold by resisting the magnetic attraction that runs between lovers.

"But soft! What light through yonder window breaks? It is east and Juliet is the sun!"

There is another - and this is relatively vague to be honest - quality to the scene and indeed story, which alludes to a sad state of affairs I think we all privately acknowledge; Juliet is not happy at home. Why exactly is hard to tell. She's got an ice-queen for a mum – we'll get to that later – and her dad is your typical flamboyant, extravagant, charismatic, passionate Italian mafia bull head – we'll get to that later as well– but even from these early scenes we can see a certain eagerness to leave it all behind and elope with her true love. *"And all my fortunes at thy foot I'll lay, and follow thee my lord throughout the world,"* she says and she certainly means it. What this all suggests is something abundantly clear in the general use of her language; Romeo is her shining knight in armour and has come to sweep her away from a dull and closeted world, which she yearns to escape from to a life of adventure. Of course this is no great revelation, but later on we will see how this current 'family designed path' she's confined to will become a terrible woe for Juliet and it is nice to see that Shakespeare gave us fair warning from the start, he knew where it was all going and he connects everything up like one of those children's colouring books where you draw lines between two columns and all the different lines cross and overlap each other and to find the connection you have to trace the line with your finger between to the two entries... ...know what I mean? The simply comical, incessant, crescendoing calls for Juliet that the Nurse screams out like a barbarian every few seconds say it all.

Friar Laurence's chiding about Rosaline – gotta love that. He's so damn blasphemous! *"Benedicte!... ...Holy Saint Francis!... ...Jesu Maria!"* Banging on and on, telling Romeo how shameless he is and then suddenly – snap! - the idea dawns on him, like an epiphany; he can use their love to bring the families together! Sounds like a plan anyway. And then later on, when he weds them, did you hear the thunder rolling in the distance again as the good friar so cringingly broached the truth, saying *"These violent delights have violent ends and in their triumph die, like fire and powder, which as they kiss consume,"* ?

There is this terribly disturbing moment, when the Nurse dances a fine line between black humour and grim reality, saying *"I anger her sometimes and tell her that Paris is the properer man; but, I'll warrant you, when I say so, she looks as pale as any clout,"* I don't know about you, but I don't even want to hear that creep's name. Ugh. But that's just the Nurse isn't it? A rambling, foolish old woman who just waffles on about anything that pops into her head and has no regard for time nor tact. Still, she's got her heart in the right place. Mostly.

For now, we are left we the charming image of these two young people enjoying the best moments of their life so far. They're in complete ecstasy. When they say 'yes' you know they really mean it. In sickness, in health and even in death they will be united. Caution: those with a weak heart to stop reading now.

THE
MOST EX=
cellent and lamentable
Tragedie, of Romeo
and *Iuliet*.

Newly corrected, augmented, and
amended:

As it hath bene sundry times publiquely acted, by the
right Honourable the Lord Chamberlaine
his Seruants.

LONDON
Printed by Thomas Creede, for Cuthbert Burby, and are to
be sold at his shop neare the Exchange.
1599.

ACT III

Verona, the town square.
Enter Mercutio, Benvolio,
Page & Servants attending

Out in the street, Mercutio, Benvolio and their crew kick it in the midsummer heat of July...

Benvolio

I pray thee, good Mercutio, let's retire:
The day is hot, the Capulets abroad,
And, if we meet, we shall not scape a brawl;
For now, these hot days, is the mad blood stirring.

I beg you, good Mercutio, let's turn in: the day is hot, the Capulets are on their movements and, if we meet, we will not escape without a fight: because now, in these hot days, the madness in the blood is beginning to stir.

Mercutio

Thou art like one of those fellows that when he enters the confines of a tavern claps me his sword upon the table and says 'God send me no need of thee!' and by the operation of the second cup draws it on the drawer, when indeed there is no need.

You are like one of those fellas that when he enters the pub throws his sword down on the table and says [to the sword:] 'God send me no need of you!' and then, by the operation of a second cup of wine, draws his sword on the bartender, when indeed there is no need.

Benvolio

Am I like such a fellow?

Is that what I'm like yeah?

Mercutio

Come, come, thou art as hot a Jack in thy mood as any in Italy, and as soon moved to be moody, and as soon moody to be moved.

Come, come, you are as hot-headed a Jack when you're in a mood as any in Italy (*we are in Verona, Italy*) and you are as quick to be in a mood as when you are in a mood to be moved [to fight] (*Mercutio is really describing himself*).

Benvolio

And what to?

And what [is it that moves me] to [fight]?

Mercutio

Nay, an there were two such, we should have none shortly, for one would kill the other. Thou! why, thou wilt quarrel with a man that hath a hair more, or a hair less, in his beard, than thou hast: thou wilt quarrel with a man for cracking nuts, having no other reason but because thou hast hazel eyes: what eye but such an eye would spy out such a quarrel? Thy head is as full of quarrels as an egg is full of meat, and yet thy head hath been beaten as addle as an egg for quarrelling: thou hast quarrelled with a man for coughing in the street, because he hath wakened thy dog that hath lain asleep in the sun: didst thou not fall out with a tailor for wearing his new doublet before Easter? with another, for tying his new shoes with old riband? and yet thou wilt tutor me from quarrelling!

Na, if there were *two* people like you we should have none soon, for they would kill each other. You! Why, you will quarrel with a man that has a hair more or a hair less in his beard than you have: you will quarrel with a man for cracking nuts, having no other reason but because you have hazel eyes (*1. hazel the colour brown 2. hazelnuts like in a chocolate bar*): what eye other than such an eye as yours would spy out such a quarrel? Your head is as full of quarrels as an egg is full of (*meat : fleshy food*) and despite that your head has been beaten like a scrambled egg for quarrelling: you have quarrelled with a man for coughing in the street because he woke up your dog that was lying asleep in the sun: didn't you fall out with a tailor for wearing his new jacket before Easter (*because during lent we should fast and not be getting nice new things*)? With another, for tying his new shoes with an old ribbon? And yet you try and encourage me not to fight!

Benvolio

An I were so apt to quarrel as thou art, any man should buy the fee-simple of my life for an hour and a quarter. By my head, here come the Capulets!

If I was so ready to fight as you are, any person would probably buy the contract of my life within an hour and a quarter. By my head, here come the Capulets!

Mercutio

By my heel, I care not.

Enter Tybalt & Others

Original	Modern
Tybalt *Follow me close, for I will speak to them.* *Gentlemen, good den: a word with one of you.* **Mercutio** *And but one word with one of us? Couple it* *with something; make it a word and a blow.* **Tybalt** *You shall find me apt enough to that, sir,* *an you will give me occasion.* **Mercutio** *Could you not take some occasion without giving?* **Tybalt** *Mercutio, thou consort'st with Romeo-* **Mercutio** *Consort! what, dost thou make us minstrels?* *An thou make minstrels of us, look to hear nothing* *but discords: here's my fiddlestick; here's that shall* *make you dance. 'Zounds, consort!*	Make sure you've got my back, for I will speak to them. Gentlemen, good afternoon! A word with one of you. Just one word with one of us? Couple it with something; make it a word and blow [*1. a punch* *2. a rude sexual suggestion*] You will find I am ready enough for that if you give me a reason. Could you not take some reason without me giving? Mercutio, you consort [*1. deal, have a relationship...*] with Romeo- [*2. consort : old word for a music band*]! What, do you think we're musicians? And you make musicians of us, looking to hear nothing but [*1. discord : upset 2. dis-chords, wrong-notes*]: here's my fiddle [*sword*] that will make you dance! Zounds, consort! [*Zounds is a common phrase meaning 'goodness me!', originally deriving from a shortened 'Christ's wounds'*]
Benvolio *We talk here in the public haunt of men:* *Either withdraw unto some private place,* *And reason coldly of your grievances,* *Or else depart; here all eyes gaze on us.* **Mercutio** *Men's eyes were made to look, and let them* *gaze; I will not budge for no man's pleasure, I.*	We talk here in public: either we should fall back to some private place and calmly discuss your grievances or else leave: here all eyes look at us. Men's eyes were made to look and let them gaze; I will not budge for no man's pleasure, I.
Enter Romeo **Tybalt** *Well, peace be with you, sir: here comes my man.* **Mercutio** *But I'll be hanged, sir, if he wear your livery:* *Marry, go before to field, he'll be your follower;* *Your worship in that sense may call him 'man.'*	Well, peace be with you sir, he comes my man. I'll be hanged sir, if he wears your [*livery : uniform*] colours [*Your man?*]: mind you, go into a field [*to fight with him*] and he will 'follow you': you can compliment him in that sense and call him 'man'.
Tybalt *Romeo, the love I bear thee can afford* *No better term than this: thou art a villain.* **Romeo** *Tybalt, the reason that I have to love thee* *Doth much excuse the appertaining rage* *To such a greeting: villain am I none;* *Therefore farewell; I see thou know'st me not.*	Romeo, the love I have for you can achieve no better term than this: you are an evil b***ard. Tybalt, the reason that I have to love you does much excuse the rage belonging to such a greeting: evil b***ard am I not; therefore, farewell, I see you don't know me.
Tybalt *Boy, this shall not excuse the injuries* *That thou hast done me; therefore turn and draw.* **Romeo** *I do protest, I never injured thee,* *But love thee better than thou canst devise,*	Boy, that will not excuse the injuries that you have done to me: therefore, turn and draw! I do protest, I never injured you but love you better than you can imagine,

51

Till thou shalt know the reason of my love:
And so, good Capulet - which name I tender
As dearly as my own - be satisfied.

Mercutio

O calm, dishonourable, vile submission!
Alla stoccata carries it away.

                              [Draws]
          Tybalt, you rat-catcher, will you walk?

Tybalt

          What wouldst thou have with me?

Mercutio

          Good King of Cats, nothing but one of your
nine lives; that I mean to make bold withal, and as
you shall use me hereafter, drybeat the rest of the
eight. Will you pluck your sword out of his Pilcher
by the ears? make haste, lest mine be about your
ears ere it be out.

Tybalt

          I am for you.

                              [Drawing]

Romeo

          Gentle Mercutio, put thy rapier up.

Mercutio

          Come, sir, your passado.

          They fight bravely.
          Romeo is unarmed and
          appeals to Benvolio:

Romeo

          Draw, Benvolio; beat down their weapons.
Gentlemen, for shame, forbear this outrage!
Tybalt, Mercutio, the Prince expressly hath
Forbidden bandying in Verona streets:
Hold, Tybalt! good Mercutio!

          Romeo steps between them.
          Tybalt stabs Mercutio under Romeo's arm
          then flies with his followers

Mercutio

          I am hurt. A plague o' both your houses! I am
sped. Is he gone, and hath nothing?

Benvolio

          What, art thou hurt?

Mercutio

          Ay, ay, a scratch, a scratch; marry, 'tis
enough. Where is my page?
          Go, villain, fetch a surgeon.

                              [Exit Page]

Romeo

          Courage, man; the hurt cannot be much.

---

until you know the reason for my love: and so,
good Capulet - which name I care about as dearly
as my own - be satisfied.

Oh, calm, dishonourable, vile submission! [*Alla
stoccata : the opening move in fencing*] finishes
the fight! [*Drawing his sword*] Tybalt, you kitten,
will you walk the walk?

What do you want with me?

Good king of cats, nothing but one of your nine
lives that I will do as I please with and as you will
know about hereafter, [*drybeat : beat without
drawing blood*] the other eight out of you. Will
you pluck your sword out of his [*pilcher :
scabbard*] by the ears? Make haste, in case
mine is around your ears before it be out.

Gentle Mercutio, put your [*rapier : type of sword*]
away!

Come, sir, your [*passado : lunge*]

Draw, Benvolio; beat down their weapons.
Gentlemen, for shame, hold-back this outrage!
Tybalt, Mercutio, the Prince has expressly
forbidden sword-fights in Verona's streets. Hold
Tybalt! Good Mercutio!

*With Romeo trying to step between them, Tybalt
stabs Mercutio and then runs off with his crew.*

I am hurt. A plague on both your houses! I am
done for [*sped : dispatched to heaven where the
soul speeds to*]. Is he gone and has no injury of
his own?

What, are you hurt?

Yeah, yeah, a scratch, a scratch; mind you, it is
enough. Where's my runner? Go, rascal, fetch a
surgeon.

Courage man, the hurt cannot be much.

Mercutio

No, 'tis not so deep as a well, nor so wide as a church-door; but 'tis enough, 'twill serve: ask for me to-morrow, and you shall find me a grave man. I am peppered, I warrant, for this world. A plague o' both your houses! 'Zounds, a dog, a rat, a mouse, a cat, to scratch a man to death! a braggart, a rogue, a villain, that fights by the book of arithmetic! Why the devil came you between us? I was hurt under your arm.

Romeo

I thought all for the best.

Mercutio

Help me into some house, Benvolio, Or I shall faint. A plague o' both your houses! They have made worms' meat of me: I have it, And soundly too: your houses!

Romeo

This gentleman, the Prince's near ally, My very friend, hath got his mortal hurt In my behalf; my reputation stain'd With Tybalt's slander - Tybalt, that an hour Hath been my kinsman! O sweet Juliet, Thy beauty hath made me effeminate And in my temper soften'd valour's steel!

Benvolio

O Romeo, Romeo, brave Mercutio's dead! That gallant spirit hath aspired the clouds, Which too untimely here did scorn the earth.

Romeo

This day's black fate on more days doth depend; This but begins the woe, others must end.

Benvolio

Here comes the furious Tybalt back again.

Romeo

Alive, in triumph! and Mercutio slain! Away to heaven, respective lenity, And fire-eyed fury be my conduct now!
[Enter Tybalt; Romeo retrieves Mercutio's sword from the dust]
Now, Tybalt, take the villain back again, That late thou gavest me; for Mercutio's soul Is but a little way above our heads, Staying for thine to keep him company: Either thou, or I, or both, must go with him.

Tybalt

Thou, wretched boy, that didst consort him here,
Shalt with him hence.

Romeo

This shall determine that.

They engage; In combat, Romeo uses his dagger and stabs Tybalt in the heart; Tybalt falls

No, it's not as deep as a well or as wide as a church-door; but it is enough, it will serve: ask for me tomorrow and you will find me a grave man [1. grave as in grumpy 2. grave as in dead]. I am peppered [seasoned and ready to cook], I tell you, ready to leave this world. A plague on both your houses! Zounds, a dog, a rat, a mouse, a cat to scratch a man to death! A show-off, a rogue, a villain that fights by the book of numbers [Tybalt fights without any imagination]! Why the devil did you come between us? I was hurt under your arm.

Help me into some house, Benvolio, or I will faint. A plague on both your houses! They have made meat to feed the worms out of me: I know it, and well too: [curse] your houses!

This gentleman, the Prince's confidant, my true friend, has got his mortal hurt on my behalf; my reputation stained with Tybalt's slander – Tybalt, that just one hour has been my family! Oh, sweet Juliet, your beauty has made me act like a female and in my temper [1. nature 2. how you make a sword :] softened valour's steel!

Oh Romeo, Romeo, brave Mercutio's dead! That noble spirit has risen to the clouds which going at the wrong time has bitterly scorned our world.

This day's black fate isn't finished yet: this only begins the troubles that others must end.

Alive and in triumph! And Mercutio killed! Away to heaven, considerate gentleness and let fire-eyed fury be my behaviour now!

Now, Tybalt, take back when you called me a 'villain' because Mercutio's soul is but a little way above our heads, waiting for you to keep him company. Either you or I or both must go with him [to the afterlife].

You wretched boy that did roll with him that's dead here, will go with him there.

[his sword]

Benvolio

Romeo, away, be gone! The citizens are up,
and Tybalt slain. Stand not amazed: the Prince will
doom thee death,
If thou art taken: hence, be gone, away!

Romeo

O, I am fortune's fool!

Benvolio

Why dost thou stay?

[Exit Romeo]

Enter Citizens

First Citizen

Which way ran he that kill'd Mercutio?
Tybalt, that murderer, which way ran he?

Benvolio

There lies that Tybalt.

First Citizen

Up, sir, go with me;
I charge thee in the Prince's name, obey.

Enter Prince, attended by Guard;
Montague & Capulet, their wives and others

Prince

Where are the vile beginners of this fray?

Where are the disgraceful beginners of this
conflict?

Benvolio

O noble Prince, I can discover all
The unlucky manage of this fatal brawl:
There lies the man, slain by young Romeo,
That slew thy kinsman, brave Mercutio.

Oh noble Prince, I can reveal all the unlucky
happenings of this fatal brawl: there lies the man,
slain by young Romeo that killed your family,
brave Mercutio. (*n.b. It is not ever made clear
how exactly Mercutio and the Prince are related
in case you thought you missed something*)

Lady Capulet

Tybalt, my cousin! O my brother's child!
O Prince! O cousin! husband! O, the blood is spilt
O my dear kinsman! Prince, as thou art true,
For blood of ours, shed blood of Montague.
O cousin, cousin!

Tybalt, my cousin! Oh my brother's child! Oh
Prince! Oh cousin! Husband! Oh, the blood is spilt,
oh my dear kinsman! Prince, as you are true, for
blood of ours, shed blood of Montague. Oh
cousin, cousin!

Prince

Benvolio, who began this bloody fray?

Benvolio

Tybalt, here slain, whom Romeo's hand did slay;
Romeo that spoke him fair, bade him bethink
How nice the quarrel was, and urged withal
Your high displeasure: all this uttered
With gentle breath, calm look, knees humbly bow'd,
Could not take truce with the unruly spleen
Of Tybalt deaf to peace, but that he tilts
With piercing steel at bold Mercutio's breast,
Who all as hot, turns deadly point to point,
And, with a martial scorn, with one hand beats
Cold death aside, and with the other sends
It back to Tybalt, whose dexterity,

Tybalt, killed here, was slain by Romeo's hand;
Romeo spoke to him fair, asked him to think
twice about how good an idea the quarrel was
and urged that you would be greatly upset: all
this he said with a gentle voice, calm look, knees
humbly bowed but he could not convince the
(*spleen : ill-temper*) of Tybalt, deaf to peace, who
then points his piercing steel at bold Mercutio's
breast, who just as hot-headed, turns his own
deadly point to point back at him and with a war-
like scorn, with one hand beats cold death aside
and with the other sends it back to Tybalt, who
with precision

Retorts it: Romeo he cries aloud,
'Hold, friends! friends, part!' and, swifter than his
tongue, his agile arm beats down their fatal points,
And 'twixt them rushes; underneath whose arm
An envious thrust from Tybalt hit the life
Of stout Mercutio, and then Tybalt fled;
But by and by comes back to Romeo,
Who had but newly entertain'd revenge,
And to 't they go like lightning, for, ere I
Could draw to part them, was stout Tybalt slain.
And, as he fell, did Romeo turn and fly.
This is the truth, or let Benvolio die.

Lady Capulet

He is a kinsman to the Montague;
Affection makes him false; he speaks not true:
Some twenty of them fought in this black strife,
And all those twenty could but kill one life.
I beg for justice, which thou, Prince, must give;
Romeo slew Tybalt, Romeo must not live.

Prince

Romeo slew him, he slew Mercutio;
Who now the price of his dear blood doth owe?

Montague

Not Romeo, Prince, he was Mercutio's friend;
His fault concludes but what the law should end,
The life of Tybalt.

Prince

And for that offence
Immediately we do exile him hence:
I have an interest in your hate's proceeding,
My blood for your rude brawls doth lie a-bleeding;
But I'll amerce you with so strong a fine
That you shall all repent the loss of mine:
I will be deaf to pleading and excuses;
Nor tears nor prayers shall purchase out abuses:
Therefore use none: let Romeo hence in haste,
Else, when he's found, that hour is his last.
Bear hence this body and attend our will:
Mercy but murders, pardoning those that kill.

Exeunt

retaliates. Romeo cries aloud 'Hold friends! Friends, part!' and swifter than his tongue, uses his arm to beat down their fatal points rushing between them; underneath his arm Tybalt thrust a hit on the life of brave Mercutio and then Tybalt fled. But by and by he comes back to Romeo, who now wanted revenge and to it they go like lightning and before I could draw them apart brave Tybalt was slain. And, as he fell, Romeo turned and ran away. This is the truth or let Benvolio die.

He is a kinsman to the Montague: affection makes him false; he's lying. Some twenty of them fought in this black strife and all those twenty could only kill one life. I beg for justice, which you, Prince, must give; Romeo killed Tybalt, Romeo must not live.

Romeo killed him, he killed Mercutio; who now will pay the price of his dear blood?

Not Romeo, Prince, he was Mercutio's friend; his mistake finishes but what the law should end; the life of Tybalt.

And for that offence I immediately exile him from here: I have an interest in what your hate is making happen, my blood (*Mercutio*), because of your rude brawls, lies here bleeding; but I will (*amerce : fine*) you with so strong a fine that you will regret this loss of mine. I will be deaf to pleading and excuses; not tears, not prayers will be able to buy out your punishment. Therefore, use none; let Romeo go from here quickly, or else, when he's found, that hour is his last. Take from here this body and do as I say: Mercy only murders more people when pardoning those that kill.

55

III.II

Enter Juliet alone

Juliet

Gallop apace, you fiery-footed steeds,
Towards Phoebus' lodging: such a wagoner
As Phaëthon would whip you to the west,
And bring in cloudy night immediately.
Spread thy close curtain, love-performing night,
That runaway's eyes may wink and Romeo
Leap to these arms, untalk'd of and unseen.
Lovers can see to do their amorous rites
By their own beauties; or, if love be blind,
It best agrees with night. Come, civil night,
Thou sober-suited matron, all in black,
And learn me how to lose a winning match,
Play'd for a pair of stainless maidenhoods:
Hood my unmann'd blood, bating in my cheeks,
With thy black mantle; till strange love, grown bold,
Think true love acted simple modesty.
Come, night; come, Romeo; come, thou day in night;
For thou wilt lie upon the wings of night
Whiter than new snow on a raven's back.
Come, gentle night, come, loving, black-brow'd night,
Give me my Romeo; and, when he shall die,
Take him and cut him out in little stars,
And he will make the face of heaven so fine
That all the world will be in love with night
And pay no worship to the garish sun.
O, I have bought the mansion of a love,
But not possess'd it, and, though I am sold,
Not yet enjoy'd: so tedious is this day
As is the night before some festival
To an impatient child that hath new robes
And may not wear them. O, here comes my nurse,
And she brings news; and every tongue that speaks
But Romeo's name speaks heavenly eloquence.

Enter Nurse w cords

Now, Nurse, what news? What hast thou there?
     The cords that Romeo bid thee fetch?

Nurse

Ay, ay, the cords.

                              [*Putting them down*]

Juliet

Ay me! what news? why dost thou wring thy hands?

Nurse

Ah, well-a-day! he's dead, he's dead, he's dead!
We are undone, lady, we are undone!
Alack the day! he's gone, he's kill'd, he's dead!

Juliet

Can heaven be so envious?

Gallop quickly, you [*fiery-footed steeds : the horses drawing Helios' chariot*], towards Phoebus' [*Pheobus : Latin name of Apollo*] house [*bring on sunset*]: the same as if Phaëthon [*Apollo's son who rode the chariot for a day but couldn't control it and so was killed by Zeus*] was whipping you [*the horses pulling the sun*] to the west and bring in cloudy night immediately. Close your curtains, love-performing night so that runaway's eyes [*in the sense of people's eyes who are out of control and always looking around*] will sleep and let Romeo leap into these arms, untalked of and unseen. Lovers can see to do their loving rituals by their own powers [*because lover's eyes were often thought of as shining out light*]; or, if love is blind, it best goes with night. Come, civil night, you severely dressed matron, all in black, and teach me how to lose a winning match played for a pair of unstained virginities: Hood my uncontrolled blood [*like a hawk is hooded to calm it down*], blushing in my cheeks, with your black cover; until cautious love, grown bold, thinks of sex as a simple and modest activity. Come, night, come Romeo, come you day in night; for you will lie upon the wings of night whiter than new snow on a raven's back. Come, gentle night, come, loving black-brow'd night, give me my Romeo; and, when he dies, take him and cut him out in little stars and he will make the face of heaven so fine that all the world will be in love with night and pay no worship to the tacky sun. Oh, I have bought the mansion of a love but not possessed it and although I am sold, not yet enjoyed. So tedious is this day like the night before some festival to an impatient child that has new robes and is not allowed to wear them. Oh, here comes my nurse and she brings news; and every tongue that speaks Romeo's name speaks heavenly eloquence.

Enter Nurse with rope-ladder

Now, Nurse, what news? What have you there? The rope-ladder that Romeo asked you to get?

Yes, yes, the rope-ladder.

Goodness me! What news? Why do you wring your hands?

Ah, alas! He's dead, he's dead, he's dead! We are undone, lady, we are undone! Alas the day! He's gone, he's killed, he's dead!

Can heaven be so jealous [*as to kill Romeo*]?!

56

Come civil night,
Thou sober-suited
matron, all in black,
And learn me how to
lose a winning match,
Play'd for a pair of
stainless maidenhoods:

Nurse

Romeo can, though heaven cannot: O Romeo,
Romeo! Who ever would have thought it? Romeo!

Juliet

What devil art thou, that dost torment me thus?
This torture should be roar'd in dismal hell.
Hath Romeo slain himself? say thou but 'I,'
And that bare vowel 'I' shall poison more
Than the death-darting eye of cockatrice:
I am not I, if there be such an I;
Or those eyes shut, that make thee answer 'I.'
If he be slain, say 'I'; or if not, no:
Brief sounds determine of my weal or woe.

(Romeo was 'envious' enough to kill Tybalt)

What devil are you, that does torment me so?
This torture should be used in hell. Has Romeo
slain himself? Say you but [*I : ay : yes*] and that
single vowel 'I' will poison me more than the
death-darting eye of the [*cockatrice : mythical
beast that killed you the instant you looked it in
the eye*]. I [*Juliet*] am not I if there be such an I [*if
there be such a word that tells me Romeo is
dead*] or those eyes are shut that make you
answer ' I '. If he be slain, say ' I ' or if not ' no' :
brief sounds will decide between my great
happiness or terrible pain.

Nurse

I saw the wound, I saw it with mine eyes,
- God save the mark! - here on his manly breast:
A piteous corse, a bloody piteous corse;
Pale, pale as ashes, all bedaub'd in blood,
All in gore-blood; I swounded at the sight.

Juliet

O, break, my heart! poor bankrupt, break at once!
To prison, eyes, ne'er look on liberty!
Vile earth, to earth resign; end motion here;
And thou and Romeo press one heavy bier!

I saw the wound, I saw it with my eyes – God
save the mark! [*an expression meaning 'God
save us from this calamity', see appendix*] – here
on his manly breast: a pitiful corpse, a bloody
pitiful corpse, pale, pale as ashes, all covered in
blood, all in gory blood: I passed out at the sight.

Oh, break my heart! Poor and bankrupt, break at
once! To prison send my eyes, never to look on
freedom again! Disgusting world, to earth
commit [my body]; end the motion of living here
and you [*her body*] and Romeo can push up
thorns [*similar to 'push up daisies' as we might
say today*] [together].

Nurse

O Tybalt, Tybalt, the best friend I had!
O courteous Tybalt! Honest gentleman!
That ever I should live to see thee dead!

Juliet

What storm is this that blows so contrary?
Is Romeo slaughter'd, and is Tybalt dead?
My dear-loved cousin, and my dearer lord?
Then, dreadful trumpet, sound the general doom!
For who is living, if those two are gone?

Nurse

Tybalt is gone and Romeo banished;
Romeo that kill'd him, he is banished.

Juliet

O God! did Romeo's hand shed Tybalt's blood?

Nurse

It did, it did; alas the day, it did!

Juliet

O serpent heart, hid with a flowering face!
Did ever dragon keep so fair a cave?
Beautiful tyrant! fiend angelical!
Dove-feather'd raven! wolvish-ravening lamb!
Despised substance of divinest show!
Just opposite to what thou justly seem'st,
A damned saint, an honourable villain!

What storm is this that blows in the opposite
direction? Is Romeo slaughtered and is Tybalt
dead? My dear-loved cousin and my dearer lord?
Then, dreadful trumpet [*of judgement day*] sound
the general doom! For who is living, if those two
are gone?

(banished : exiled)

O serpent heart, hid with a flowering face! Was
there ever a dragon that lived in so beautiful a
cave? Beautiful tyrant! Angel-like fiend! Raven
with a dove's feathers! Lamb that eats like the
wolf! Despised substance that looked divine! Just
opposite to what you rightly seemed, a damned
saint, an honourable villain!

O nature, what hadst thou to do in hell,
When thou didst bower the spirit of a fiend
In moral paradise of such sweet flesh?
Was ever book containing such vile matter
So fairly bound? O that deceit should dwell
In such a gorgeous palace!

Nurse
There's no trust, No faith, no honesty in men;
all perjured, All forsworn, all naught, all dissemblers.
Ah, where's my man? give me some aqua vitae:
These griefs, these woes, these sorrows make me old.
Shame come to Romeo!

Juliet
Blister'd be thy tongue For such a wish! he
was not born to shame: Upon his brow shame is
ashamed to sit; For 'tis a throne where honour may be
crown'd Sole monarch of the universal earth.
O, what a beast was I to chide at him!

Nurse
Will you speak well of him that kill'd your cousin?

Juliet
Shall I speak ill of him that is my husband?
Ah, poor my lord, what tongue shall smooth thy
name, when I, thy three-hours wife, have mangled it?
But, wherefore, villain, didst thou kill my cousin?
That villain cousin would have kill'd my husband:
Back, foolish tears, back to your native spring;
Your tributary drops belong to woe,
Which you, mistaking, offer up to joy.
My husband lives, that Tybalt would have slain;
And Tybalt's dead, that would have slain my
husband: All this is comfort; wherefore weep I then?
Some word there was, worser than Tybalt's death,
That murder'd me: I would forget it fain;
But, O, it presses to my memory,
Like damned guilty deeds to sinners' minds:
'Tybalt is dead, and Romeo - banished;'
That 'banished,' that one word 'banished,'
Hath slain ten thousand Tybalts. Tybalt's death
Was woe enough, if it had ended there:
Or, if sour woe delights in fellowship
And needly will be rank'd with other griefs,
Why follow'd not, when she said 'Tybalt's dead,'
Thy father, or thy mother, nay, or both,
Which modern lamentations might have moved?
But with a rear-ward following Tybalt's death,
'Romeo is banished,' to speak that word,
Is father, mother, Tybalt, Romeo, Juliet,
All slain, all dead. 'Romeo is banished!'
There is no end, no limit, measure, bound,
In that word's death; no words can that woe sound.
Where is my father, and my mother, Nurse?

Oh nature, what would you be doing in hell,
considering that you have lodged the spirit of a
demon in a perfectly-moral man, made of such
sweet flesh? Was ever a book, containing such
vile subject-matter, so fairly bound? Oh that
deceit should dwell in such a gorgeous palace!

There's no trust, no faith, no honesty in men: all
are liars, all are denouncers of their oaths, all are
nothing, all are disguised. Ah, where's my man
[*Peter*]? Get me some alcoholic-spirits, these
griefs, these woes, these sorrows make me old.
Shame come to Romeo!

Blistered be your tongue for such a wish! He was
not born to shame: upon his brow shame is
ashamed to sit; for it is a throne where honour
may be crowned sole monarch of the universal
earth. Oh, what a beast was I to hate on him!

Will you speak well of him that killed your cousin?

Will I talk ill of him that is my husband? Ah, my
poor lord, what tongue will smooth your name,
when I, your three-hours wife, have mangled it?
But for what reason, villain, did you kill my
cousin? That villain cousin would have killed my
husband: back, foolish tears, back to your native
spring; your [*tributary : where rivers divide*] drops
[*of water/tears*] belong to woe, which you,
mistaking, offer up to joy. My husband lives, that
Tybalt would have slain; and Tybalt's dead, that
would have slain my husband. All this is comfort,
so why should I cry then? Some word there was,
worse than Tybalt's death, that murdered me: I
would forget it willingly, but oh, it presses to my
memory like damned guilty deeds to a sinner's
mind: Tybalt is dead and Romeo – banished. That
'banished' that one word 'banished' has slain ten
thousand Tybalts. Tybalt's death was woe
enough, if it had ended there: or, if sour woe
loves to have company and needs to be ranked
with other griefs, why didn't it follow when she
said 'Tybalt's dead', your father or your mother,
no, or both which would have moved me to
ordinary mourning? But with [*rear-ward : a
defensive position in a retreating army*] following
Tybalt's death, 'Romeo is banished' to speak that
word is father, mother, Tybalt, Romeo, Juliet, all
slain, all dead. 'Romeo is banished!' there is no
end, no limit, no measure, boundary, in that
word's death. No words can describe that woe.
Where is my father and my mother Nurse? [*Nb.
It's not like today, there were no mobile phones
or e-mail. Romeo's banishment probably means
Juliet will never see him again*]

Nurse

　　Weeping and wailing over Tybalt's corse:
Will you go to them? I will bring you thither.

Juliet

　　Wash they his wounds with tears: mine shall be
spent, when theirs are dry, for Romeo's banishment.
Take up those cords: poor ropes, you are beguiled,
Both you and I; for Romeo is exiled:
He made you for a highway to my bed;
But I, a maid, die maiden-widowed. Come, cords,
come, Nurse; I'll to my wedding-bed; and Death, not
Romeo, take my maidenhead!

Nurse

　　Hie to your chamber: I'll find Romeo
To comfort you: I wot well where he is.
Hark ye, your Romeo will be here at night:
I'll to him; he is hid at Laurence' cell.

Juliet

　　O, find him! give this ring to my true knight,
And bid him come to take his last farewell.

　　　　　　　　　　　　　　　　　Exeunt

Weeping and wailing over Tybalt's corpse. Will
you go to them? I will bring you there.

They wash his wounds with tears: mine will be
spent when theirs are dry, for Romeo's
banishment. Take up that rope-ladder: poor
ropes, you are cheated, both you and I; for
Romeo is exiled: he made you for a highway to
my bed. But I, a maid, die a virgin-widow. Come,
ropes, come Nurse: I'll to my wedding-bed and
death not Romeo, take my virginity!

Get to your chamber: I'll find Romeo to comfort
you: I know well where he is. Listen you, your
Romeo will be here at night: I'll to him; he is hid at
Friar Laurence's cell.

Oh, find him! Give this ring to my true knight and
bid him come to take his last farewell.

O SERPENT HEART, HID WITH A FLOWERING FACE! DID EVER DRAGON KEEP SO FAIR A CAVE? BEAUTIFUL TYRANT! FIEND ANGELICAL! DOVE-FEATHER'D RAVEN! WOLVISH-RAVENING LAMB!

III.III

Friar Laurence's cell.
Enter Friar Laurence

Friar Laurence
Romeo, come forth; come forth, thou fearful man:
Affliction is enamour'd of thy parts,
And thou art wedded to calamity.

Romeo, come out here; come out here you fearful man: Suffering is attracted to your nature and you are married to catastrophe.

Enter Romeo

Romeo
Father, what news? what is the prince's doom?
What sorrow craves acquaintance at my hand,
That I yet know not?

Father, what news? What is the Prince's punishment? What sorrow desires to meet my hand that I do not know of yet?

Friar Laurence
Too familiar
Is my dear son with such sour company:
I bring thee tidings of the prince's doom.

My dear son is too familiar with such sour problems: I bring you news of the Prince's judgement.

Romeo
What less than dooms-day is the prince's doom?

What punishment less than dooms-day is the prince's sentencing?

Friar Laurence
A gentler judgment vanish'd from his lips,
Not body's death, but body's banishment.

A less-severe judgement vanished from his lips (*because once spoken, our words vanish*), not body's death (*you will not die*) but body's banishment (*you are exiled from Verona*).

Romeo
Ha, banishment! be merciful, say 'death;'
For exile hath more terror in his look,
Much more than death: do not say 'banishment.'

Friar Laurence
Hence from Verona art thou banished:
Be patient, for the world is broad and wide.

Romeo
There is no world without Verona walls,
But purgatory, torture, hell itself.
Hence banished is banish'd from the world,
And world's exile is death: then banished,
Is death mis-term'd: calling death banishment,
Thou cutt'st my head off with a golden axe,
And smilest upon the stroke that murders me.

There is no world outside of Verona's walls, only purgatory, torture, hell itself. Therefore banished is banished from the world, and the world's exile is death: then banished is death termed incorrectly: calling death banishment, you cut off my head with a golden axe and smile on the stroke that murders me.

Friar Laurence
O deadly sin! O rude unthankfulness!
Thy fault our law calls death; but the kind prince,
Taking thy part, hath rush'd aside the law,
And turn'd that black word death to banishment:
This is dear mercy and thou seest it not.

O deadly sin! O rude unthankfulness! What you did the law says you should die for; but the kind prince, taking your side, has brushed aside the law and turned that black word 'death' into 'banishment': this is dear mercy and you can't see it.

Romeo
'Tis torture, and not mercy: heaven is here,
Where Juliet lives; and every cat and dog
And little mouse, every unworthy thing,
Live here in heaven and may look on her;
But Romeo may not: more validity,

It is torture and not mercy; heaven is here where Juliet lives and every cat and dog and little mouse, every unworthy thing can live here in heaven and can look upon her; but Romeo may not! More value,

61

More honourable state, more courtship lives
In carrion-flies than Romeo: they may seize
On the white wonder of dear Juliet's hand
And steal immortal blessing from her lips,
Who even in pure and vestal modesty,
Still blush, as thinking their own kisses sin;
But Romeo may not; he is banished:
Flies may do this, but I from this must fly:
They are free men, but I am banished.
And say'st thou yet that exile is not death?
Hadst thou no poison mix'd, no sharp-ground knife,
No sudden mean of death, though ne'er so mean,
But 'banished' to kill me? 'Banished'?
O friar, the damned use that word in hell;
Howlings attend it: how hast thou the heart,
Being a divine, a ghostly confessor,
A sin-absolver, and my friend profess'd,
To mangle me with that word 'banished'?

Friar Laurence
    Thou fond mad man, hear me but speak a word.

Romeo
    O, thou wilt speak again of banishment.

Friar Laurence
    I'll give thee armour to keep off that word:
Adversity's sweet milk, philosophy,
To comfort thee, though thou art banished.

Romeo
    Yet 'banished'? Hang up philosophy!
Unless philosophy can make a Juliet,
Displant a town, reverse a prince's doom,
It helps not, it prevails not: talk no more.

Friar Laurence
    O, then I see that madmen have no ears.

Romeo
    How should they, when that wise men have no eyes?

Friar Laurence
    Let me dispute with thee of thy estate.

Romeo
    Thou canst not speak of that thou dost not feel:
Wert thou as young as I, Juliet thy love,
An hour but married, Tybalt murdered,
Doting like me and like me banished,
Then mightst thou speak, then mightst thou tear thy
hair, and fall upon the ground, as I do now,
Taking the measure of an unmade grave.

                       [Knocking within]

Friar Laurence
    Arise; one knocks; good Romeo, hide thyself.

Romeo
    Not I; unless the breath of heartsick groans,
Mist-like, infold me from the search of eyes.

---

more honour, more charm lives in [*carrion-flies :
flies that feed on meat i.e. ordinary flies*] than in
Romeo [because] they are allowed to claim land
on the white wonder of dear Juliet's hand and
steal immortal blessing from her lips, who even
in pure and virgin modesty, still blush, for thinking
their own kisses [*flies landing on her lips*] a sin;
but Romeo may not; he is banished; flies may do
this but I from this must fly: they are free men
but I am banished. And you still say that exile is
not death? Haven't you got no poison mixed, no
sharp-[*ground on a whet-stone*] knife, no sudden
means of death, no matter how primitive but
'banished' with which to kill me? 'Banished'? Oh
friar, the damned souls in hell use that word;
howling goes with it: how have you the heart,
being a religious minister, a spiritual councillor,
an absolver of sins and declare yourself my dear
friend, to mangle me with the word 'banished'?

You foolish mad man, listen to what I'm trying to
tell you for one second.

I'll give you armour to defend you from that word:
hardship's sweet milk, philosophy [*from hardship
we cipher philosophy which is nourishing and
precious*], to comfort you although you are
banished.

Still 'banished'? Forget philosophy! Unless
philosophy can make Juliet transplant a town [or]
reverse a prince's sentence, it helps not, it wins
not: talk no more.

Oh, then I see that madmen have no ears.

How should they, when wise [*old*] men [*such as
Friar Laurence*] have no eyes [*to see what's
going on*]?

Let me argue with you about your state of affairs.

You cannot speak of what you do not feel: if you
were as young as I, Juliet your love, married for
only an hour, Tybalt murdered, loving like me and
like me banished, then you could speak, then you
could tear your hair and fall upon the ground as I
do now, taking the measurements of an un-dug
grave.

Get up, someone's knocking; good Romeo, hide
yourself.

Not I; unless the breath of heartsick groans, like
a mist, enfold me from the sight of eyes.

[Knocking]

Friar Laurence

　　Hark, how they knock! Who's there? Romeo, arise;
Thou wilt be taken. Stay awhile! Stand up;

[Knocking]

Run to my study. By and by! God's will,
What simpleness is this! I come, I come!
Who knocks so hard? whence come you?
　　　　　　　　　　what's your will?

Nurse [Within]

　　Let me come in, and you shall know my errand;
　　　　　　　I come from Lady Juliet.

Friar Laurence

　　Welcome, then.

Listen, how they knock! Who's there? Romeo, get
up, you will be taken. Wait a minute! Stand up;

　　　　　Enter Nurse

Nurse

　　O holy friar, O, tell me, holy friar,
Where is my lady's lord, where's Romeo?

Friar Laurence

　　There on the ground, with his own tears made drunk.

Nurse

　　O, he is even in my mistress' case,
Just in her case! O woeful sympathy!
Piteous predicament! Even so lies she,
Blubbering and weeping, weeping and blubbering.
Stand up, stand up; stand, an you be a man:
For Juliet's sake, for her sake, rise and stand;
Why should you fall into so deep an O?

Romeo

　　Nurse!

Nurse

　　Ah sir! ah sir! Well, death's the end of all.

Romeo

　　Spakest thou of Juliet? how is it with her?
Doth she not think me an old murderer,
Now I have stain'd the childhood of our joy
With blood removed but little from her own?
Where is she? and how doth she? and what says
My conceal'd lady to our cancell'd love?

Nurse

　　O, she says nothing, sir, but weeps and weeps;
And now falls on her bed; and then starts up,
And Tybalt calls; and then on Romeo cries,
And then down falls again.

Romeo

　　As if that name, Shot from the deadly level of a gun,
Did murder her; as that name's cursed hand
Murder'd her kinsman. O, tell me, friar, tell me,
In what vile part of this anatomy
Doth my name lodge? Tell me, that I may sack
The hateful mansion.　　　　　[Drawing his sword]

Oh, he is in the same state as my mistress, just
in her state! Oh woeful sympathy! Piteous
predicament! Just like that she lies, blubbering
and weeping, weeping and blubbering. Stand up,
stand up; stand, if you be a man: for Juliet's sake,
for her sake, rise and stand: Why should you fall
into so deep an [O : the noise we make when we
groan in sincere woe]?

['death's the end of all' : a phrase meaning 'well it
can't be all that bad']

Are you talking about Juliet? How is it with her?
Does she not think of me as an old murderer,
now I have stained the childhood of our joy with
blood removed a little way [in her family] from her
own? Where is she? And how does she? And
what says my secret lady to our [cancell'd : a
legal term] ' voided ' love?

Oh, she says nothing, sir, but weeps and weeps
and now falls on her bed and then starts up and
calls for Tybalt and then cries about Romeo and
then falls down again.

As if that name, shot from the deadly aim of a
gun, did murder her; and because that name's
cursed hand [Romeo's hand] murdered her
cousin. Oh, tell me, friar, tell me, in what vile part
of this anatomy does my name lodge? Tell me so
that I can [sack : when an army is let loose to
destroy and rob and pillage a town, for instance
'the sack of Troy'] the hateful mansion [himself].

Friar Laurence

Hold thy desperate hand:
Art thou a man? thy form cries out thou art:
Thy tears are womanish; thy wild acts denote
The unreasonable fury of a beast:
Unseemly woman in a seeming man!
Or ill-beseeming beast in seeming both!
Thou hast amazed me: by my holy order,
I thought thy disposition better temper'd.
Hast thou slain Tybalt? wilt thou slay thyself?
And slay thy lady too that lives in thee,
By doing damned hate upon thyself?
Why rail'st thou on thy birth, the heaven, and earth?
Since birth, and heaven, and earth, all three do meet
In thee at once; which thou at once wouldst lose.
Fie, fie, thou shamest thy shape, thy love, thy wit;
Which, like a usurer, abound'st in all,
And usest none in that true use indeed
Which should bedeck thy shape, thy love, thy wit:
Thy noble shape is but a form of wax,
Digressing from the valour of a man;
Thy dear love sworn but hollow perjury,
Killing that love which thou hast vow'd to cherish;
Thy wit, that ornament to shape and love,
Misshapen in the conduct of them both,
Like powder in a skitless soldier's flask,
Is set afire by thine own ignorance,
And thou dismember'd with thine own defence.

What, rouse thee, man! thy Juliet is alive,
For whose dear sake thou wast but lately dead;
There art thou happy: Tybalt would kill thee,
But thou slew'st Tybalt; there are thou happy too:
The law that threaten'd death becomes thy friend
And turns it to exile; there art thou happy:
A pack of blessings lights up upon thy back;
Happiness courts thee in her best array;
But, like a mishaped and sullen wench,
Thou pout'st upon thy fortune and thy love:
Take heed, take heed, for such die miserable.
Go, get thee to thy love, as was decreed,
Ascend her chamber, hence and comfort her:
But look thou stay not till the watch be set,
For then thou canst not pass to Mantua;
Where thou shalt live, till we can find a time
To blaze your marriage, reconcile your friends,
Beg pardon of the prince, and call thee back
With twenty hundred thousand times more joy
Than thou went'st forth in lamentation.
Go before, Nurse: commend me to thy lady;
And bid her hasten all the house to bed,
Which heavy sorrow makes them apt unto:
Romeo is coming.

Hold your desperate hand: are you a man? The way you look says you are: your tears are womanish, your wild acts suggest the unreasonable fury of a beast: indecent woman for looking like a man! Or disgustingly-indecent beast in pretending to be both [*a woman looking like a man*]! You have amazed me: by my holy order I thought your temper was better controlled. Have you slain Tybalt? Will you slay yourself? And slay your lady too that lives in you, by doing damned hate upon yourself? Why do you hate on your own birth, the heaven and earth? Since birth, and heaven and earth, all three do live in you at once; which you at once would like to lose. Damn, damn, you shame your body, your love, your intelligence; which, like a [*usurer : a greedy money lender*], you horde and use none in that good use which should decorate your body, your love, your intelligence. Your noble shape is but a wax-figure, running away from the valour of a man: your dear love sworn is but hollow perjury, killing that love which you have vowed to cherish. Your intellect, that source of pride dedicated to being and love, is deformed in how you use both, like gun-powder in the skittish soldier's flask [*which he would pour into a gun normally*] is set aflame by your own ignorance and you are blown to shreds with your own defence [*old guns, prior to flint-locks, used matches to ignite the gun powder and fire a bullet. For this reason, it was very dangerous*].

What, awake you, man! Your Juliet is alive, for whose dear sake you were dead but a moment ago, there are you happy: Tybalt would kill you but you killed Tybalt; there are you happy too. The law that threatened death becomes your friend and turns it into exile; there are you happy. A pack of blessings sits upon your back; happiness courts you in her best clothes, but, like she were an ugly and grumpy wench, you sneer at your fortune and your love: take heed, take heed, for such people die miserable. Go, get you to your love as was decided [*before all the upset with Tybalt*], climb to her chamber, go there and comfort her: but make sure you do not stay past when the night-watch starts for then you will not be able to go to Mantua where you will live until we can find a time to re-ignite your marriage, reconcile your friends, beg pardon of the prince and call you back with twenty hundred thousand times more joy than you went away in sadness. Go ahead of him, Nurse: send my love to your lady [*in this case, Lady Capulet not Juliet*] and tell her to hurry everyone to bed, which heavy sorrow [*for Tybalt's death*] would only be appropriate for them to do. Romeo is coming.

64

Nurse

O Lord, I could have stay'd here all the night
To hear good counsel: O, what learning is!
My lord, I'll tell my lady you will come.

Oh Lord, I could have stayed here all night to hear [your] good advice: oh, what a joy learning is! My lord, I'll tell my lady you will come.

Romeo

Do so, and bid my sweet prepare to chide.

Do so and bid my sweet prepare to tell me off.

Nurse

Here, sir, a ring she bid me give you, sir:
Hie you, make haste, for it grows very late.
[Exit Nurse]

Romeo

How well my comfort is revived by this!

Friar Laurence

Go hence; good night; and here stands all your
state: either be gone before the watch be set,
Or by the break of day disguised from hence:
Sojourn in Mantua; I'll find out your man,
And he shall signify from time to time
Every good hap to you that chances here:
Give me thy hand; 'tis late: farewell; good night.

Go from here; good night and here is the only thing you should worry about: either be gone before the night-watch begins or by the break of day, in a disguise, go from here: hang around in Mantua; I'll find your main man and he will let you know from time to time every good happening for you that occurs here: give me your hand; it is late, farewell, good night.

Romeo

But that a joy past joy calls out on me,
It were a grief, so brief to part with thee: Farewell.
                                                    Exeunt

If it weren't for a joy beyond joy calls out for me, I would be upset, so soon, to part from you: farewell.

HOLD THY DESPERATE HAND: ART THOU A MAN?

III.IV

Capulet's Mansion.
Enter Capulet & Lady Capulet and Paris

Capulet

    Things have fall'n out, sir, so unluckily,
That we have had no time to move our daughter:
Look you, she loved her kinsman Tybalt dearly,
And so did I. Well, we were born to die.
'Tis very late, she'll not come down to-night:
I promise you, but for your company,
I would have been a-bed an hour ago.

Paris

    These times of woe afford no time to woo.
Madam, good night: commend me to your daughter.

Lady Capulet

    I will, and know her mind early to-morrow;
To-night she is mew'd up to her heaviness.

Capulet

    Sir Paris, I will make a desperate tender
Of my child's love: I think she will be ruled
In all respects by me; nay, more, I doubt it not.
Wife, go you to her ere you go to bed;
Acquaint her here of my son Paris' love;
And bid her, mark you me, on Wednesday next
        -But, soft! what day is this?

Paris

    Monday, my lord.

Capulet

    Monday! ha, ha! Well, Wednesday is too soon,
O' Thursday let it be: o' Thursday, tell her,
She shall be married to this noble earl.
Will you be ready? do you like this haste?
We'll keep no great ado, a friend or two;
For, hark you, Tybalt being slain so late,
It may be thought we held him carelessly,
Being our kinsman, if we revel much:
Therefore we'll have some half a dozen friends,
And there an end. But what say you to Thursday?

Paris

    My lord, I would that Thursday were to-morrow.

Capulet

    Well get you gone: o' Thursday be it, then.
Go you to Juliet ere you go to bed,
Prepare her, wife, against this wedding-day.
Farewell, my lord. Light to my chamber, ho!
Afore me! it is so very very late,
That we may call it early by and by.
Good night.

                    Exeunt

Things have fallen out, sir, so unluckily, that we have had no time to convince our daughter: look you, she loved her cousin Tybalt dearly and so did I. Well, we were born to die. It's very late, she won't come down tonight. I promise you, if it wasn't for your company, I would have gone to bed an hour ago [*notice how his thoughts jump around, perhaps Capulet is drunk*].

These times of woe afford no time to woo. Madam, good night: commend me to your daughter.

I will and I'll find out what she thinks [about you marrying her] early tomorrow; tonight she is [*mew : cage for falcons*] caged in her heaviness.

Sir Paris, I will make a bold tender of my child's love: I think she will be ruled in all respects by me; nay, more, I doubt it not. Wife, go you to her before you go to bed; remind her of my son here, Paris' love and bid her, you listen closely to me, on Wednesday next – But wait! What day is it today [*perhaps Capulet is very drunk*]?

Monday! Ha, ha! Well, Wednesday is too soon, on Thursday let it be: on Thursday, tell her, she shall be married to this noble earl. Will you be ready? Do you like this haste? We'll make no great fuss, a friend or two; for, listen you, Tybalt being slain so recently it may be thought we held him carelessly, being our kinsman, if we have too much fun: therefore, we'll have some half a dozen friends and that's all. But what say you to Thursday?

My lord, I wish that Thursday was tomorrow.

Well, get you gone: on Thursday it will be then. [*To Lady Capulet:*] You go to Juliet before you go to bed, prepare her, wife, for this wedding-day. Farewell, my lord. Light to my chamber, ho [*whenever Shakespeare has his characters say 'light... ho!' he means that character is commanding his minions to light the way for him*]! Goodness me! It is so very, very late that we may call it early by and by. Good night.

III.V

Capulet Mansion.
Enter Romeo & Juliet,
at her chamber window

Juliet

    Wilt thou be gone? It is not yet near day:
It was the nightingale, and not the lark,
That pierced the fearful hollow of thine ear;
Nightly she sings on yon pomegranate-tree:
Believe me, love, it was the nightingale.

Romeo

    It was the lark, the herald of the morn,
No nightingale: look, love, what envious streaks
Do lace the severing clouds in yonder east:
Night's candles are burnt out, and jocund day
Stands tiptoe on the misty mountain tops.
I must be gone and live, or stay and die.

Juliet

    Yon light is not day-light, I know it, I:
It is some meteor that the sun exhales,
To be to thee this night a torch-bearer,
And light thee on thy way to Mantua:
Therefore stay yet; thou need'st not to be gone.

Romeo

    Let me be ta'en, let me be put to death;
I am content, so thou wilt have it so.
I'll say yon grey is not the morning's eye,
'Tis but the pale reflex of Cynthia's brow;
Nor that is not the lark, whose notes do beat
The vaulty heaven so high above our heads:
I have more care to stay than will to go:
Come, death, and welcome! Juliet wills it so.
How is't, my soul? let's talk; it is not day.

Juliet

    It is, it is: hie hence, be gone, away!
It is the lark that sings so out of tune,
Straining harsh discords and unpleasing sharps.
Some say the lark makes sweet division;
This doth not so, for she divideth us:
Some say the lark and loathed toad change eyes,
O, now I would they had changed voices too!
Since arm from arm that voice doth us affray,
Hunting thee hence with hunt's-up to the day,
O, now be gone; more light and light it grows.

Romeo

    More light and light; more dark and dark our woes!

Enter Nurse

Nurse

    Madam!

Will you be gone? It is not yet near day: it was the nightingale and not the lark that pierced the fearful hollow of your ear; nightly she sings on that pomegranate-tree: believe me, love, it was the nightingale [*it is true that nightingales choose a tree to sing in, staying there until scared off, sometimes for weeks on end*].

It was the lark, the herald of the morning, no nightingale: look, love, what envious streaks of light do lace the parting clouds that way east: night's candles [*the stars*] are burnt out and cheerful day stands tiptoe on the misty mountain tops. I must be gone and live or stay and die.

That light is not day-light, I know it, I: it is some meteor that the sun exhales in order to be for you a torch-bearer tonight and light you on your way to Mantua [*another town in Italy*]: therefore stay for now, you need not be gone.

Let me be taken, let me be put to death; I am content if that's what you want. I'll say that grey is not the morning's eye, it is but the pale reflection of (*Cynthia : the moon goddess*)'s brow [*a cloud*]. Neither is that the lark, whose notes do echo in the spacious heaven so high above our heads: I have more care to stay than will to go: come, death, and welcome! Juliet wills it so. How do you like that, my soul? Let's talk; it is not day.

It is, it is: quickly go, be gone, away! It is the lark that sings so out of tune, straining to reach harsh chords and unpleasant high-notes. Some say the lark makes sweet work of it; this is not so, for she divides us. Some say the lark and loathed toad exchanged eyes [*because the ugly toad has big beautiful eyes and the beautiful lark has nasty little beady eyes*] oh, now I wish they had changed voices too [*so that the lark would grimly croak the arrival of morning and suit the situation better*]! Since arm from arm that voice does scare [*us away from each other*], hunting you away with [*hunt's-up : music played to wake people up on special occasions e.g. before a hunt, the day of a wedding etc.*] to the day, oh, now be gone: more light and light it grows.

Juliet

  Nurse?

Nurse

  Your lady mother is coming to your chamber:
  The day is broke; be wary, look about.

                                              [Exit Nurse]

Juliet

  Then, window, let day in and let life out.

Romeo

  Farewell, farewell! One kiss, and I'll descend.

                              [He goeth down] (*Romeo climbs down from her balcony.*)

Juliet

  Art thou gone so? love, lord, ay, husband, friend!   Art you gone so? Love, lord, yes, husband, friend!
  I must hear from thee every day in the hour,   I must hear from you every day on the hour for in
  For in a minute there are many days: a minute there are many days. Oh, by this count I
  O, by this count I shall be much in years   shall be very old before I hold my Romeo again!
  Ere I again behold my Romeo!

Romeo

  Farewell! I will omit no opportunity   Farewell! I will miss no opportunity to send my
  That may convey my greetings, love, to thee.   greetings, love, to you.

Juliet

  O think'st thou we shall ever meet again?   Oh do you think we will ever meet again?

Romeo

  I doubt it not; and all these woes shall serve   I doubt it not; and all these woes will serve for
  For sweet discourses in our time to come.   sweet discussions in our time to come.

Juliet

  O God, I have an ill-divining soul!   Oh God, my soul senses something terrible! I
  Methinks I see thee, now thou art below,   thought to myself, now you are below, [that you
  As one dead in the bottom of a tomb: looked] like a person dead in the bottom of a
  Either my eyesight fails, or thou look'st pale.   tomb: either my eyesight fails or you look pale.

Romeo

  And trust me, love, in my eye so do you: And trust me, love, in my eye so do you: dry
  Dry sorrow drinks our blood. Adieu, adieu!   sorrow drinks our blood. (*Adieu : Latin for 'To*
                                                           God' meaning goodbye)
                                [Exit Romeo]

Juliet

  O fortune, fortune! all men call thee fickle: Oh fortune, fortune! All men call you bitchy: if you
  If thou art fickle, what dost thou with him   are so erratic, what will you do with him (*Romeo*)
  That is renown'd for faith? Be fickle, fortune;   that is renowned for his faith? Be volatile,
  For then, I hope, thou wilt not keep him long,   fortune, for then, I hope, you will not keep him
  But send him back.   long but send him back.

Lady Capulet *[Within]*

  Ho, daughter! Are you up?

Juliet

  Who is't that calls? is it my lady mother?   Who is that who calls? Is it my lady mother? Is
  Is she not down so late, or up so early?   she not gone to bed, so late or is she up early?
  What unaccustom'd cause procures her hither?   What unusual reason brings about her coming?

                    Enter Lady Capulet

Lady Capulet

  Why, how now, Juliet!

Juliet

Madam, I am not well.

Lady Capulet

Evermore weeping for your cousin's death?
What, wilt thou wash him from his grave with tears?
An if thou couldst, thou couldst not make him live;
Therefore, have done: some grief shows much of love;
But much of grief shows still some want of wit.

Juliet

Yet let me weep for such a feeling loss.

Lady Capulet

So shall you feel the loss, but not the friend
Which you weep for.

Juliet

Feeling so the loss,
Cannot choose but ever weep the friend.

Lady Capulet

Well, girl, thou weep'st not so much for his death,
As that the villain lives which slaughter'd him.

Juliet

What villain madam?

Lady Capulet

That same villain, Romeo.

Juliet [Aside]

-Villain and he be many miles asunder -
God pardon him! I do, with all my heart;
And yet no man like he doth grieve my heart.

Lady Capulet

That is, because the traitor murderer lives.

Juliet

Ay, madam, from the reach of these my hands:
Would none but I might venge my cousin's death!

Lady Capulet

We will have vengeance for it, fear thou not:
Then weep no more. I'll send to one in Mantua,
Where that same banish'd runagate doth live,
Shall give him such an unaccustom'd dram,
That he shall soon keep Tybalt company:
And then, I hope, thou wilt be satisfied.

Juliet

Indeed, I never shall be satisfied
With Romeo, till I behold him -dead-
Is my poor heart for a kinsman vex'd.
Madam, if you could find out but a man
To bear a poison, I would temper it;
That Romeo should, upon receipt thereof,
Soon sleep in quiet. O, how my heart abhors
To hear him named, and cannot come to him
To wreak the love I bore my cousin
Upon his body that slaughter'd him!

Still crying for your cousin's death? What, will you wash him from his grave with tears? And even if you could, you could not make him live; therefore, [*have done : finish*]. Some grief shows much of love; but too much grief shows some lack of intellect.

But let me cry for such a feeling of loss.

All you're doing is feeling the loss but not the friend who you weep for.

Feeling the loss I do, I cannot choose but to forever weep for the friend.

Well, girl, you weep not so much for his death as that villain who lives that slaughtered him.

- The term 'Villain' and Romeo are many miles apart – God pardon him! I do, with all my heart; and yet no man like he does make my heart sad.

That is because the treacherous murderer lives.

Yes, madam, he lives out of reach of these, my hands: I wish none but myself might revenge my cousin's death!

We will have vengeance for it, do not fear: so stop crying. I'll send message to one in Mantua, where that same banished renegade does live, who will give him an unusual drink [*poison*], so that he will soon be keeping Tybalt company: and then, I hope, you will be satisfied.

Indeed, 1. I never shall be satisfied with Romeo until I see him 2. I never shall be satisfied with Romeo until I see him dead 3. dead [*uncaring*] is my heart for a cousin [*Tybalt*] who got pissed off. Madam, if you could just find out a man to deliver a poison, I would mix it so that Romeo should, upon receiving it, soon sleep in quiet [*she is lying, she would diffuse the poison not make it stronger*]. Oh, how my heart is disgusted to hear him named and I cannot come to him to unleash the love I had for my cousin upon his body that slaughtered him [*1. violently attack him 2. have vigorous sex with him*]!

Lady Capulet

Find thou the means, and I'll find such a man.
But now I'll tell thee joyful tidings, girl.

You find a way and I'll find the man for the job.
But now I'll tell you good news, girl.

Juliet

And joy comes well in such a needy time:
What are they, I beseech your ladyship?

And joy comes well in such a needy time: what is
the news, I beg to know your ladyship?

Lady Capulet

Well, well, thou hast a careful father, child;
One who, to put thee from thy heaviness,
Hath sorted out a sudden day of joy,
That thou expect'st not nor I look'd not for.

Well, well, you have a caring father, child: one
who, to put you from your heaviness, has sorted
out a sudden day of joy that you didn't expect and
neither did I look for.

Juliet

Madam, in happy time, what day is that?

Lady Capulet

Marry, my child, early next Thursday morn,
The gallant, young and noble gentleman,
The County Paris, at Saint Peter's Church,
Shall happily make thee there a joyful bride.

By Mary, my child, early next Thursday morning,
the gallant, young and noble gentleman, the
(*County : Count*) Paris, at Saint Peter's Church,
will happily make you a joyful bride there.

Juliet

Now, by Saint Peter's Church and Peter too,
He shall not make me there a joyful bride.
I wonder at this haste; that I must wed
Ere he, that should be husband, comes to woo.
I pray you, tell my lord and father, madam,
I will not marry yet; and, when I do, I swear,
It shall be Romeo, whom you know I hate,
Rather than Paris. These are news indeed!

Now, by Saint Peter's Church and Peter too he
shall not make me there a joyful bride. I wonder
at this haste; that I must wed before he, that's
going to be my husband, has even come to woo. I
beg you, tell my lord and father, madam, I will not
marry yet and when I do, I swear, it will be with
Romeo whom you know I hate rather than Paris.
This is news indeed!

Lady Capulet

Here comes your father; tell him so yourself,
And see how he will take it at your hands.

Enter Capulet and Nurse

Capulet

When the sun sets, the air doth drizzle dew;
But for the sunset of my brother's son
It rains downright. How now! a conduit, girl? what,
still in tears? Evermore showering? In one little body
Thou counterfeit'st a bark, a sea, a wind;
For still thy eyes, which I may call the sea,
Do ebb and flow with tears; the bark thy body is,
Sailing in this salt flood; the winds, thy sighs;
Who, raging with thy tears, and they with them,
Without a sudden calm, will overset
Thy tempest-tossed body. How now, wife!
Have you deliver'd to her our decree?

When the sun sets, the air does drizzle dew; but
for the sunset of my brother's son (*Tybalt*) it
rains outright. How now! A fountain girl? What,
still in tears? Evermore showering? In one little
body you have the image of a ship, a sea, a wind;
for still your eyes, which I may call the sea, do
ebb and flow with tears; the ship is your body,
sailing in this salt flood; the winds are you sighs,
who, raging with tears and they with them, with
no sudden calm in the storm, will capsize your
tempest-tossed body. How now, wife! Have you
delivered to her our decision?

Lady Capulet

Ay, sir; but she will none, she gives you
thanks. I would the fool were married to her grave!

Yes, sir, although she doesn't want anything to
do with it, gives you thanks. I would the fool were
married to her grave!

Capulet

Soft! Take me with you, take me with you, wife.
How will she none? doth she not give us thanks?
Is she not proud? doth she not count her blest,

Shh! Let me understand, let me understand this,
wife. How? Will she none? Does she not give us
thanks? Is she not proud? Does she not count

Unworthy as she is, that we have wrought
So worthy a gentleman to be her bridegroom?

Juliet

Not proud, you have; but thankful, that you
have: Proud can I never be of what I hate;
But thankful even for hate, that is meant love.

Capulet

How now, how now, chop-logic! What is this?
'Proud,' and 'I thank you,' and 'I thank you not;'
And yet 'not proud,' mistress minion, you,
Thank me no thankings, nor, proud me no prouds,
But fettle your fine joints 'gainst Thursday next,
To go with Paris to Saint Peter's Church
or I will drag thee on a hurdle thither.
Out, you green-sickness carrion! out, you baggage!
You tallow face!

Lady Capulet [to husband]

Fie, fie! what, are you mad?

Juliet

Good father, I beseech you on my knees,
Hear me with patience but to speak a word.

Capulet

Hang thee, young baggage! disobedient
wretch! I tell thee what: get thee to church o'
Thursday, or never after look me in the face:
Speak not, reply not, do not answer me;
My fingers itch. Wife, we scarce thought us blest
That God had lent us but this only child;
But now I see this one is one too much,
And that we have a curse in having her:
Out on her, hilding!

Nurse

God in heaven bless her! You are to blame, my
lord, to rate her so.

Capulet

And why, my lady wisdom? hold your tongue,
Good prudence; smatter with your gossips, go.

Nurse

I speak no treason.

Capulet

O, God ye god-den.

Nurse

May not one speak?

Capulet

Peace, you mumbling fool!
Utter your gravity o'er a gossip's bowl,
    for here we need it not.

Lady Capulet

You are too hot.

Capulet

God's bread! it makes me mad:
Day, night, hour, tide, time, work, play,

her blessings, unworthy that she is, that we have fashioned such a worthy gentlemen to be her bridegroom?

Not proud you have but thankful that you have. Proud I could never be of that which I hate; but thankful even for hate that is meant in love.

How now, how now, mixed-up-logic! What is this? 'Proud' and 'I thank you' and 'I thank you not' and yet 'not proud', my little mistress you thank me no thankings, nor proud me no prouds just brace-up your bones in time for next Thursday to go with Paris to Saint Peter's Church or I will drag you there on a sledge. Out, you green-sickness of rotting meat [*because she is unmarried she is getting ill and her body is rotting like meat*]! Out, you impudent girl! You pale-face!

Good father, I beg of you on my knees, hear me with patience speak just a few words.

Hang you, young harlot! Disobedient wretch! I tell you what: get you to church on Thursday or never look me in the face again: speak not, reply not, do not answer me; my fingers itch [to slap you]. Wife, we always thought we were blessed that God had sent us but this only child; but now I see this one is one too much and that we have a curse in having her; out on her, worthless person!

God in heaven bless her! You are to blame, my lord, to criticise her so.

And why, my lady wisdom? Hold your tongue with great care; chatter with your gossips, go.

I haven't said anything treacherous.

Oh, God give a good evening [*goodbye*]!

Peace, you mumbling fool! Speak your wisdom over a bowl of soup with your gossip-friends for here we need it not.

God's bread [*Christ's flesh*]! It makes me mad; day, night, hour, tide, time, work, play,

Alone, in company, still my care hath been
To have her match'd: and having now provided
A gentleman of noble parentage,
Of fair demesnes, youthful, and nobly train'd,
Stuff'd, as they say, with honourable parts,
Proportion'd as one's thought would wish a man;
And then to have a wretched puling fool,
A whining mammet, in her fortune's tender,
To answer 'I'll not wed; I cannot love,
I am too young; I pray you, pardon me.'
But, as you will not wed, I'll pardon you:
Graze where you will you shall not house with me:
Look to't, think on't, I do not use to jest.
Thursday is near; lay hand on heart, advise:
An you be mine, I'll give you to my friend;
And you be not, hang, beg, starve, die in
the streets, for, by my soul, I'll ne'er acknowledge
thee, nor what is mine shall never do thee good:
Trust to't, bethink you; I'll not be forsworn.

[Exit Capulet]

alone, in company, always my priority has been to have her matched; and now I have provided a gentleman of noble parentage, of fair wealth, youthful and well trained, stuffed as they say with honourable qualities, proportioned as one's thought would wish a man; and then to have a wretched whimpering fool, a whining play-doll, when her fortune's going well, to answer 'I'll not wed, I cannot love, I am too young, I pray you, pardon me.' But, as you will not wed, I'll pardon you: graze wherever you want you will not live with me: look to it, think on it, I do not joke. Thursday is near, lay hand on heart, think hard: if you be mine, I'll give you to my friend and if you be not [mine], hang, beg, starve, die in the streets for by my soul I'll never acknowledge you, nor what is mine shall ever do you good. Trust to it, think about it; I'll not be made to break my word.

Juliet

Is there no pity sitting in the clouds,
That sees into the bottom of my grief?
O, sweet my mother, cast me not away!
Delay this marriage for a month, a week;
Or, if you do not, make the bridal bed
In that dim monument where Tybalt lies.

Is there no pity sitting in the clouds that sees the depth of my grief? Oh, sweet mother, don't throw me out! Delay this marriage for a month, a week; or, if you do not, make the bridal bed in that dim monument where Tybalt lies.

Lady Capulet

Talk not to me for I'll not speak a word:
Do as thou wilt, for I have done with thee.

[Exit Lady Capulet]

Talk not to me for I'll not speak a word:
Do as you will, for I am finished with you.

Juliet

O God! O Nurse, how shall this be prevented?
My husband is on earth, my faith in heaven;
How shall that faith return again to earth,
Unless that husband send it me from heaven
By leaving earth? comfort me, counsel me.
Alack, alack, that heaven should practise stratagems
Upon so soft a subject as myself!
What say'st thou? hast thou not a word of joy?
Some comfort, Nurse.

Oh God! Oh, Nurse, how will this be prevented? My husband is on earth, my faith in heaven; how will that faith return again to earth unless that husband sent it to me from heaven by leaving earth? Comfort me, advise me. Alas, alas, that heaven should practise strategies upon so soft a subject as myself! What say you? Have you not a word of joy? Some comfort, Nurse.

Nurse

Faith, here it is. Romeo is banish'd; and all the
world to nothing, that he dares ne'er come back to
challenge you; or, if he do, it needs must be by stealth.
Then, since the case so stands as now it doth,
I think it best you married with the county.
O, he's a lovely gentleman! Romeo's a dishclout to
him: an eagle, madam, hath not so green, so quick, so
fair an eye as Paris hath. Beshrew my very heart,
I think you are happy in this second match,
For it excels your first: or if it did not,

Faith, here it is. Romeo is banished and [*all the world to nothing : the odds, i.e. it's a safe bet*] that he won't dare come back to claim you; or, if he does, it needs to be in secret. Then, since the situation stands as it does, I think it's best you marry with the count [*Paris*]. Oh he's a lovely gentlemen! Romeo's a dish-cloth to him: an eagle, madam has not so fresh, quick, so fair an eye as Paris has. Excuse my very heart, I think you are happier in this second match for it excels your first or if it did not

Your first is dead; or 'twere as good he were,
As living here and you no use of him.
Juliet
    Speakest thou from thy heart?
Nurse
  And from my soul too; Or else beshrew them both.
Juliet
    Amen!
Nurse
    What?
Juliet
    Well, thou hast comforted me marvellous
much. Go in: and tell my lady I am gone,
Having displeased my father, to Laurence' cell,
To make confession and to be absolved.
Nurse
    Marry, I will; and this is wisely done.
                  [Exit Nurse]

Juliet
    Ancient damnation! O most wicked fiend!
Is it more sin to wish me thus forsworn,
Or to dispraise my lord with that same tongue
Which she hath praised him with above compare
So many thousand times? Go, counsellor;
Thou and my bosom henceforth shall be twain.
I'll to the friar, to know his remedy:
If all else fail, myself have power to die.
                        Exit

your first is dead: or it were as good as if he were, as living here you have no use of him.

Do you really mean that from your heart?

And from my soul too: or else curse them both.

So be it [*I will marry Paris/curse Nurse's soul*]!

What?

Well, you have comforted me marvellously. Go in: and tell my lady I am gone, having displeased my father, to Friar Laurence's cell to make confession and be absolved.

By Mary, I will and this is wisely done.

Ancient damnation! Oh most wicked fiend! Is it more sin to wish me break my oath [*of marriage*] or to dishonour my lord [*Romeo*] with that same tongue which she has praised him with above compare so many thousand times [*because she is constantly pretending to hate him*]? Go, counsellor [*Nurse*], you and my heart from now on will be separated. I'll go to the friar, to know his solution. If all else fail, I myself have the power to die [*commit suicide*].

How silver-sweet sound lovers' tongues by night

Commentary : Act III

Act III is The Turn. Listening to Mercutio ramble on and on about the use of over-the-top fancy-pants language – a sin which he himself is most notoriously guilty of – it is always easy for me to forget the impending catastrophe that will trigger a sequence of events eventually resulting in ruin for Juliet and her Romeo.

I have seen many Tybalts over the years – from the open air theatre in Regents Park to a Norwegian troupe performing in the Old Vic – but I can safely say I have never seen anyone portray the character so authentically as John Leguizamo in Baz Lurnham's *Romeo + Juliet, 1996*. The film overall is by no means a contender for the best ever rendition of the script, although his character has stuck in my mind particularly for his perfect mix of hard-nosed, bitter masculine pride and young buck, cheeky-chappy, having a good time. He grinds out the lines through clenched-teeth, snarling *"Romeo, the hate I bear thee can afford no better term than this: thou art a villain!"* and then he spits on the ground. Tybalt loves this sh**. He wants a showdown. But then, when the fighting really kicks off, he seems unsure of himself, running away without celebrating his victory then coming back for more like an over-excited young man.

And it is here where we discover another great vista of soul enlightening truth; mark how Romeo, newly bolstered and pumped up full of *true love*, literally overnight, has transformed from the kind of immature childish punk who would have leapt into a quarrel with Tybalt into the patient, sincere, all-embracing family visionary who we are forced to admire for so saintly denying Hate his fateful bargain. This is what true love does when it floods through the veins. It fills us from 'crown to toe-top with direst' empathy, it releases us from the chains of anxiety bound to stupid things that don't matter - in this case pride and reputation over trivial grievances – and it lets us soar above, an angel of forgiveness, capable of acquiring everything we need to make us happy without ever having to step on someone else's toes. In our world, everybody worships money and they convince themselves to do all sorts of things because they really do think it's *necessary*. But as Romeo so artfully demonstrates here, the only thing *necessary* in life is love, speaking the profoundly moving words of wisdom *"Tybalt, the reason that I have to love thee, doth much excuse the appertaining rage to such a greeting. Villain am I none; therefore, farewell, I see thou know'st me not."* This is kind of thing Bob Marley would say to someone who tried to pick a bone with him over nothing. It's humble but it's not cowardly by any measure. It's graceful, it's intelligent, it's wholesome, it's downright *superior*. It reminds me of another line from Hamlet, when he says *"Rightly to be great is not to stir without great argument,"* This idea, that we have been comprehending just now, is a gem from the very highest echelons of maturity. It will keep you safe from many disasters and it will help you become generally more relaxed in life, making way for better feelings and emotions that all contribute to a state of 'happiness'. But if you think that's clever – or cheesy – wait and see what Shakespeare does next;

Mercutio dies and he dies in such a way as it is questionable whether Romeo's 'mature actions' facilitated that death. Romeo feels responsible. I don't know about you, but it creeps me out watching Mercutio die, especially when I read it. Going back to a topic mentioned before, concerning how exactly *Romeo & Juliet* is a comedy, I find here Shakespeare really plays an elaborate prank on the audience. Watch closely; all these jokes. All this endless clowning about and stereotypes and knaves and eccentrics and wordplay makes us chuckle reading it but would have had the original Elizabethan audience in hysterics. I think Shakespeare really had his audience in uproar, I think they were drinking and laughing and every one was having a great time. And then, a sword fight! Elizabethans freakin' love sword fights! You can bet they were cheering and shouting and possibly even throwing things at Tybalt when the fight was going down. And then, everyone laughing and having a good time, it slowly emerges that Mercutio might be hurt. But he says it's just a scratch. So everyone keeps laughing. Men, women, children. And then – and I would bet fifty pounds Shakespeare gave this specific instruction to his actors at the time, that this was the exact effect he wanted – Mercutio starts saying nasty things (*"A plague on both your houses!"*), mixing it up with a kind of sick black humour that suggests to the more switched on viewers something might actually be seriously wrong (*"Ask for me tomorrow and you will find me a grave man!"*) and then he falls over and suddenly the jokes have gone out of the window. It's like how in a cheap T.V. sitcom they pull the rug of comedy out from under you and suddenly you feel all emotional and upset because of the way they flipped the script. No matter who's playing Romeo or where I'm seeing it that sentence *"I thought all for the best,"* always comes out like a sad, concerned little puppy looking up to his master because he thinks he's in trouble. The reality has yet to dawn on him but perhaps, somewhere in the recesses of his subconscious, there is the suggestion that his friend is about to die and it's his fault. Even though he did the right thing. Here, there is no corniness, there is no Hollywood think-tank philosophy demonstrating this or that. Nay, here we see events unfold as they do in real life, which often does indeed mean the good person doing the right thing and still not getting what they deserved. We're a long way from Kansas now.

Romeo's unmistakeably explosive egotistical vengeance sweeping down on Tybalt is shocking, hasty and wholly predictable. *"Either thou, or I, or both must go with him!"* Romeo screams and this time there is no messing about, it is what we lamely call 'a fight to the death' but what will always mean so much more to those contestants in that fight than it does to the casual observers. It is no surprise that the superior swordsman Tybalt, who's only real reason to fight was pride, is defeated by the relatively unskilled Romeo, full of fury for his dead friend. One might say 'it's not the size of the dog in the fight but the size of the fight in the dog'. As all this happens it's like the storm has finally broken and thunder and rain and lightning start lashing down upon us. By now, the men, women and children of Shakespeare's audience are no longer looking nervously around, hoping that things will suddenly brighten up. They, like us, are watching on in horror as their intellect catches up with their hearts.

Following this explosion we have the excruciating wait for Juliet to be told the news and then more drama as Romeo contemplates suicide with Friar Laurence. But, 'as we often see against some storm, a silence in the heavens, the rack stand-still, the bold winds speechless' [Hamlet, II.II] we enjoy a last glimmer of sunshine as the star-crossed lovers, completely intoxicated with the turbulent state of affairs they find themselves in, finally consummate their love and share a single precious night of passion together. When Romeo leaves in the morning, Juliet looks down upon him and says *"Methinks I see thee, now thou art below, as one dead in the bottom of a tomb,"* before they wrench their eyes away from each other, one last time.

'Anon the dreadful thunder doth rend the region,' moments later Juliet's parents arrive to announce she is going to be wed to the increasingly detestable Paris, in a matter of days. Say what you like about the comedy in *Romeo & Juliet*, a father saying to his daughter you can 'die in the street' should never be interpreted as funny. One of the biggest indications we have that Lady Capulet is an egotistical gold-digging wag is her inability to do anything about the situation. *"Talk not to me,"* she says coldly to her prostrating daughter, *"for I'll not speak a word."* In the light of her parent's hostility, it is disturbing to consider the implications of Juliet telling the truth. What would be done with her? She couldn't be sold off to Paris any more, although that sleaze-ball probably wouldn't mind. I mean, let's not beat around the bush here – Juliet marrying Paris would result in sexual intercourse, which clearly the girl does not want, ergo, making it, therefore, perpend, what we would call 'rape' by any modern consideration of the matter. What her parents are telling her, still with the sweat and burning kisses of her world's desire upon her wet cheek, is that she is going to be raped by Paris. Paris is going to violate her and, perhaps even worse for the insatiable empathy of the female mind, she might also fear Romeo will feel violated insofar as his betrothed will have been sexually abused by another man. For Juliet, it is just simply not an option to let that man put his hands on her. She would rather die. As soon as she is left alone with the Nurse she immediately solicits her, demanding to know the solution from one of the only adult minds she has any degree of confidence in. The Nurse has chickened out by this point and tells Juliet to forget about it, to which Juliet asks *"Speakest thou from the heart?"* and upon confirmation turns icy-cold, freezing up all over and suddenly saying she must immediately go to confession to 'absolve her sins', although it is clear by this point she has cut the Nurse out from her tiny inner-circle and will continue in the affair alone, without her best and only friend to confide in. It is disturbing to see such deathly seriousness come over such a young mind.

As we enter Act the fourth we must be aware that Juliet's last hope lies with the Friar. She has no-one else to turn to. He is her last chance. Of the few people she does know, the Friar is certainly someone she can trust. He has already jeopardised everything he has by wedding the couple. Not only is it his holy duty to keep their sacred bond intact but he must also find a way to reveal their love to the rest of the world! But he's being pushed two steps backwards, because whatever his attempt was looking like before, now Romeo has killed Tybalt it is going to be practically impossible to ever allow the families to discover the truth. What will he have to say when Juliet arrives and tells him that her parents are forcing her to marry Paris *on Thursday*? Will he know what to do? Can he *find a way*?

ACT IV

Friar Laurence's cell.
Enter Friar Laurence and Paris

Friar Laurence

On Thursday, sir? The time is very short.

Paris

My father Capulet will have it so;
And I am nothing slow to slack his haste.

My [soon-to-be]father[in-law] Capulet wants it to be like that; and I don't care to slow him down.

Friar Laurence

You say you do not know the lady's mind:
Uneven is the course, I like it not.

You say you don't know what Juliet is thinking: one-sided is this arrangement, I don't like it.

Paris

Immoderately she weeps for Tybalt's death,
And therefore have I little talk'd of love,
For Venus smiles not in a house of tears.
Now, sir, her father counts it dangerous
That she doth give her sorrow so much sway,
And in his wisdom hastes our marriage,
To stop the inundation of her tears;
Which, too much minded by herself alone,
May be put from her by society:
Now do you know the reason of this haste.

Extremely hard she cries for Tybalt's death and so I have barely talked of love, for Venus (*Venus : goddess of love a.k.a Aphrodite*) doesn't smile in a house of tears. Now, sir, her father thinks it's dangerous that she gives her sorrow so much power and in his wisdom hurries our marriage to stop the (*inundation : flooding waters*) of her tears, which worried about too much by herself, alone, may stop by spending time with others: now do you know the reason of this haste.

Friar Laurence [Aside]

I would I knew not why it should be slow'd...
Look, sir, here comes the lady towards my cell.

I wish I didn't know why it should be slowed down... Look, sir, here comes the lady towards my cell.

Enter Juliet

Paris

Happily met, my lady and my wife!

Juliet

That may be, sir, when I may be a wife.

Paris

That may be must be, love, on Thursday next.

Juliet

What must be shall be.

Friar Laurence

That's a certain text.

Paris

Come you to make confession to this father?

Juliet

To answer that, I should confess to you.

Paris

Do not deny to him that you love me.

Juliet

I will confess to you that I love him.

Paris

So will ye, I am sure, that you love me.

So you will, I am sure, tell him that you love me.

Juliet

If I do so, it will be of more price,
Being spoke behind your back, than to your face.

If I do so, it will be worth more being said behind your back than to your face.

Paris

Poor soul, thy face is much abused with tears.

Poor soul, your face is abused with tears.

Juliet

The tears have got small victory by that;
   For it was bad enough before their spite.

The tears have won a small victory by doing that,
because my face was bad enough before their
[*the tears'*] spite.

Paris

Thou wrong'st it, more than tears, with that report.

You wrong your face worse than tears by saying
that.

Juliet

That is no slander, sir, which is a truth;
   And what I spake, I spake it to my face.

It is not slander, sir, if it is the truth: and what I
said, I said it to my face [*it was not for your sake I
said that*].

Paris

Thy face is mine, and thou hast slander'd it.

Your face is mine and you have slandered it.

Juliet

It may be so, for it is not mine own.
Are you at leisure, holy father, now;
Or shall I come to you at evening mass?

That may be so, for it is not my own. Are you free,
holy father, now; or shall I come to you at
vespers?

Friar Laurence

My leisure serves me, pensive daughter, now.
My lord, we must entreat the time alone.

My free-time serves me, hard-thinking daughter,
now. My lord, we must request to spend the time
alone.

Paris

God shield I should disturb devotion!
Juliet, on Thursday early will I rouse ye:
Till then, adieu; and keep this holy kiss.
                    [*Paris kisses Juliet & departs*]

God prevent that I should interfere with devotion!
Juliet, early on Thursday I will awake you; until
then, good-bye and keep this holy kiss... mwa!
[*makes your skin crawl doesn't it?*]

Juliet

O shut the door! and when thou hast done so,
Come weep with me; past hope, past cure, past help!

Friar Laurence

Ah, Juliet, I already know thy grief;
It strains me past the compass of my wits:
I hear thou must, and nothing may prorogue it,
On Thursday next be married to this county.

Ah Juliet, I already know your problem; it strains
me past the limits of my wits: I hear you must,
and nothing may prolong it, be married to this
Count next Thursday.

Juliet

Tell me not, friar, that thou hear'st of this,
Unless thou tell me how I may prevent it:
If, in thy wisdom, thou canst give no help,
Do thou but call my resolution wise,
And with this knife [*Drawing knife*] I'll help it
presently. God join'd my heart and Romeo's, thou
our hands; Therefore, out of thy long-experienced
time, give me some present counsel, or, behold,
'Twixt my extremes and me this bloody knife
Shall play the umpire, arbitrating that
Which the commission of thy years and art
Could to no issue of true honour bring.
[*Holding knife to breast*] Be not so long to speak; I
long to die, If what thou speak'st speak not of remedy.

Don't tell me friar that you have heard of this
unless you are telling me how I might stop it from
happening: if, in your wisdom, you can give no
help then just tell me that my final decision is the
correct thing to do and with this knife I'll make it
happen [*I'll kill myself*]. God joined my heart and
Romeo's, you joined our hands [*in marriage*];
therefore, out of your long-time experience, give
me some advice immediately or, behold, between
my extreme problems [*Capulet, Lady Capulet,
Nurse & Paris etc.*] and me, this bloody knife
shall decide what's what, settling that which the
practise of your life and profession could not
bring to true honour. Don't take long to get to it; I
long to die if what you have to say is not of how to
fix this.

Friar Laurence

Hold, daughter! I do spy a kind of hope,
Which craves as desperate an execution
As that is desperate which we would prevent.
If, rather than to marry County Paris,

Wait, daughter: I do see a kind of hope which
craves as desperate an action as that which we
would like to prevent. If, rather than to marry
Count Paris

Thou hast the strength of will to slay thyself,
Then is it likely thou wilt undertake
A thing like death to chide away this shame,
That copest with death himself to scape from it:
And, if thou darest, I'll give thee remedy.

Juliet

O, bid me leap, rather than marry Paris,
From off the battlements of yonder tower; or walk in
thievish ways; or bid me lurk where serpents are;
chain me with roaring bears; or shut me nightly in a
charnel-house, o'er-cover'd quite with dead men's
rattling bones, with reeky shanks and yellow chapless
skulls; or bid me go into a new-made grave
And hide me with a dead man in his shroud;
Things that, to hear them told, have made me tremble;
And I will do it without fear or doubt,
To live an unstain'd wife to my sweet love.

Friar Laurence

Hold, then; go home, be merry, give consent
To marry Paris: Wednesday is to-morrow:
To-morrow night look that thou lie alone;
Let not thy nurse lie with thee in thy chamber:
Take thou this vial, being then in bed,
And this distilled liquor drink thou off;
When presently through all thy veins shall run
A cold and drowsy humour, which shall seize each
vital spirit; for no pulse shall keep his native progress,
but surcease: no warmth, no breath, shall testify thou
livest; the roses in thy lips and cheeks shall fade
To paly ashes, thy eyes' windows fall,
Like death, when he shuts up the day of life;
Each part, deprived of supple government,
Shall, stiff and stark and cold, appear like death:
And in this borrow'd likeness of shrunk death
Thou shalt continue two and forty hours,
And then awake as from a pleasant sleep.
Now, when the bridegroom in the morning comes
To rouse thee from thy bed, there art thou dead:
Then, as the manner of our country is,
In thy best robes thou shalt be borne to that same
ancient vault where all the kindred of the Capulets lie.
In the mean time, against thou shalt awake,
Shall Romeo by my letters know our drift,
And hither shall he come: and he and I
Will watch thy waking, and that very night
Shall Romeo bear thee hence to Mantua.
And this shall free thee from this present shame;
If no inconstant toy, nor womanish fear,
Abate thy valour in the acting it.

Juliet

Give me, give me! O, tell not me of fear!

you have the strength of will to kill yourself then it
is likely that you will do something very similar to
death to rebuke this shame, that by coping with
death himself you will escape from him; and, if
you dare, I'll give you the remedy.

Oh tell me to leap from the battlements of that
tower over there rather than marry Paris; Or tell
me to walk in a dangerous part of town, or tell
me to lurk where serpents are; chain me with
roaring bears or shut me nightly in the morgue,
covered over with dead men's rattling bones,
with stinking legs and yellow, jaw-less skulls; or
tell me to go into a new-made grave and hide me
with a dead man in his coffin; things that, to hear
them told, have made me afraid [in the past] but
now I will do without fear or doubt to live an
unstained wife for my sweet love.

Wait, then; go home, be merry, say you will marry
Paris: Wednesday is tomorrow: tomorrow night
make sure you go to bed alone; don't let your
nurse sleep with you in your chamber: take this
vial with you, then being in bed drink up this
distilled liquor; soon a cold and sleepy feeling
shall run through your veins, for no pulse will beat
it's normal rhythm, but stop: no warmth, no
breath, shall say that you are alive; the roses in
your lips and cheeks will fade to pale ashes, your
eyes window's will fall like death when he shuts
up the day of life; each part of your body will be
deprived of supple control, going stiff and stark
and cold, appearing like death: and in this
borrowed likeness of a shrinking death [*because
our bodies decay and so shrink*] you shall
continue forty two hours and then awake as from
a pleasant sleep. Now, when the bridegroom in
the morning comes to wake you from your bed,
there are you dead: then, as the manner of our
country is, in your best robes you shall be taken
to that same ancient vault where all the family of
Capulets lie. In the mean time, before you wake
up, Romeo will be told by my letters of our plan
and here shall he come and he and I will watch
your waking and that very night shall Romeo take
you away to Mantua. And this will free you from
this present shame; if no distraction, nor
womanish fear prevents your valour in the actual
doing of it.

Friar Laurence

    Hold; get you gone, be strong and prosperous
In this resolve: I'll send a friar with speed
To Mantua, with my letters to thy lord.

Juliet

    Love give me strength! and strength shall help
afford. Farewell, dear father!

                                    Exeunt

Hold it down; get you gone, be strong and make this resolve happen: I'll send a friar with speed to Mantua with the letters to your husband.

Love give me strength! And strength will help me be able to do this. Farewell, dear father!

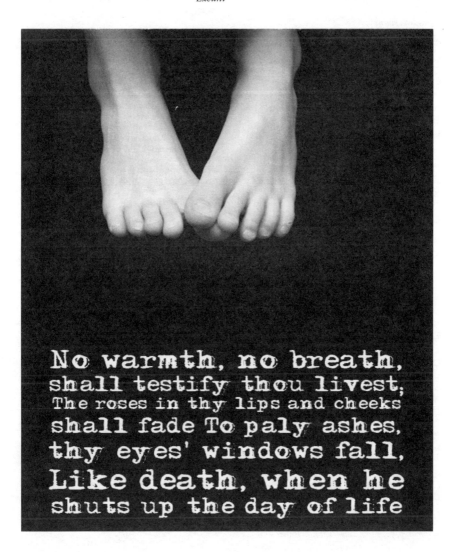

No warmth, no breath, shall testify thou livest, The roses in thy lips and cheeks shall fade To paly ashes, thy eyes' windows fall, Like death, when he shuts up the day of life

Capulet's Mansion.
Enter Capulet & Lady Capulet,
Nurse and two servants

Capulet

So many guests invite as here are writ.
[Exit First Servant]
Sirrah, go hire me twenty cunning cooks.

Invite the many guests that are written here.
[*Sirrah : used when addressing an inferior e.g.
royalty addressing their servants or as a rude
name when arguing with someone*] go and hire
twenty clever cooks.

Second Servant

You shall have none ill, sir;
for I'll try if they can lick their fingers.

You will have no bad ones sir, for as a test I'll see
if they can lick their fingers.

Capulet

How canst thou try them so?

Why exactly would you have them do that?

Second Servant

Marry, sir, 'tis an ill cook that cannot lick his
own fingers: therefore he that cannot lick his
fingers goes not with me.

By Mary, sir, it's a bad cook that cannot lick his
own fingers [*taste his own food*]: therefore
whoever can't lick their fingers won't come with
me [*i.e. taste their own medicine i.e. how would
Capulet feel if he was being made to marry
someone he didn't like?*].

Capulet

Go, be gone.
[Exit Second Servant]
We shall be much unfurnished for this time.
What, is my daughter gone to Friar Laurence?

We'll never get everything read in time. What, is
my daughter gone to see Friar Laurence?

Nurse

Ay, forsooth.

Yes, in truth.

Capulet

Well, he may chance to do some good on her:
A peevish self-will'd harlotry it is.

Well, he might do some good with her: bad-
tempered, disobedient wench that child is.

Nurse

See where she comes from shrift with merry look.

See how she comes from confession looking
merry.

Enter Juliet

Capulet

How now, my headstrong!
Where have you been gadding?

How are you, my strong-headed child! Where
have you been wandering?

Juliet

Where I have learn'd me to repent the sin
Of disobedient opposition to you and your behests,
and am enjoin'd by holy Laurence to fall prostrate
here, and beg your pardon: pardon, I beseech you!
Henceforward I am ever ruled by you.

Where I have learned to repent the sin of
disobediently opposing you [*actually, of marrying
Paris*] and your requests and I am directed by
holy Laurence to fall and bow down here and beg
your pardon: pardon, I beg you! From now on I
am always ruled by you.

Capulet

Send for the county; go tell him of this:
I'll have this knot knit up to-morrow morning.

Send for the count; go tell him of this: I'll have this
knot tied up tomorrow morning.

Juliet

I met the youthful lord at Laurence' cell;
And gave him what becomed love I might,
Not step o'er the bounds of modesty.

I met the youthful lord [*Paris*] at Laurence's cell;
and gave him the befitting love I should, not
stepping over the bounds of modesty.

Capulet

Why, I am glad on't; this is well: stand up;
This is as't should be. Let me see the county;
Ay, marry, go, I say, and fetch him hither.

Why I am glad for it; this is well; stand up; this is
as it should be. Let me see the count; ay, marry,
go, I say and bring him here.

Now, afore God! this reverend holy friar,
Our whole city is much bound to him.
Juliet
Nurse, will you go with me into my closet,
To help me sort such needful ornaments
As you think fit to furnish me to-morrow?
Lady Capulet
No, not till Thursday; there is time enough.
Capulet
Go, nurse, go with her: we'll to church to-morrow.
[Exeunt Juliet & Nurse]
Lady Capulet
We shall be short in our provision.
'Tis now near night.
Capulet
Tush, I will stir about and all things shall be
well, I warrant thee, wife: Go thou to Juliet, help to
deck up her; I'll not to bed to-night; let me alone;
I'll play the housewife for this once. What, ho!
They are all forth. Well, I will walk myself
To County Paris, to prepare him up
Against to-morrow. My heart is wondrous light,
Since this same wayward girl is so reclaim'd.
Exeunt

Now before God! This reverend holy friar, our whole city is very close to him.

Nurse, will you go with me to my bedroom to help me sort out such decorative clothes as I will need to dress in tomorrow?

No, not until Thursday, there is enough time.

Go, nurse, go with her: we'll go to church tomorrow.

We won't have everything ready: it's nearly night time.

Shh, I will move about and all things will be well, I promise you, wife. Go you to Juliet, help to dress her up; I'll not go to bed tonight, leave me alone; I'll play the housewife for once. What of it? They are all ready (*Juliet & Paris*). Well, I will walk myself to Count Paris to prepare him for tomorrow: my heart is wonderfully light since this wayward girl is so reclaimed.

IV.III

Juliet's chamber.
Enter Juliet and Nurse

Juliet

    Ay, those attires are best: but, gentle nurse,
I pray thee, leave me to my self to-night,
For I have need of many orisons
To move the heavens to smile upon my state,
Which, well thou know'st, is cross, and full of sin.

                Enter Lady Capulet

Lady Capulet

    What, are you busy, ho? Need you my help?

Juliet

    No, madam; we have cull'd such necessaries
As are behoveful for our state to-morrow:
So please you, let me now be left alone,
And let the nurse this night sit up with you;
For, I am sure, you have your hands full all,
In this so sudden business.

Lady Capulet

    Good night:
Get thee to bed, and rest; for thou hast need.

            [Exeunt Lady Capulet and Nurse]

Juliet

    Farewell! God knows when we shall meet again.
I have a faint cold fear thrills through my veins, that
almost freezes up the heat of life:
I'll call them back again to comfort me:
Nurse! What should she do here?
My dismal scene I needs must act alone.
Come, vial. What if this mixture do not work at all?
Shall I be married then to-morrow morning?
No, no: this shall forbid it: lie thou there. [Laying
down her dagger] What if it be a poison, which the
friar subtly hath minister'd to have me dead,
Lest in this marriage he should be dishonour'd,
Because he married me before to Romeo?
I fear it is: and yet, methinks, it should not,
For he hath still been tried a holy man.
How if, when I am laid into the tomb,
I wake before the time that Romeo
Come to redeem me? There's a fearful point!
Shall I not, then, be stifled in the vault,
To whose foul mouth no healthsome air breathes in,
And there die strangled ere my Romeo comes?
Or, if I live, is it not very like,
The horrible conceit of death and night,
Together with the terror of the place,
As in a vault, an ancient receptacle,
Where, for these many hundred years, the bones
Of all my buried ancestors are packed:

Yes, those garments are best: but, gentle nurse, I beg of you leave me to myself tonight for I have need of many [*orisons : prayers*] to move the heavens to smile upon my state of affairs, which, as you well know, are mixed up and full of sin.

What, are you busy? Do you need my help?

No madam, we have chosen such necessaries as are proper for our affairs tomorrow: so please you, let me now be left alone now and let the nurse keep you company tonight for I am sure you have your hands full in this very sudden business.

Good night: get you to bed and rest for you have need of it.

Goodbye! God knows when we shall meet again. I have a faint cold fear that thrills through my veins, that almost freezes up the heat of life: I'll call them back again to comfort me: Nurse! What good is she here? My dismal scene I need to act alone. Come, vial. What if this mixture does not work at all? Shall I be married then tomorrow morning? No, no: this shall prevent that (*a knife will be her last resort, to commit suicide*): lie you there [*putting the dagger down next to her bed*]. What if it is poison which the friar secretly has given to kill me because in this marriage [*to Paris*] he would be dishonoured as he already married me to Romeo? I fear it is: and yet, I think not so, for he has been tried and tested many times as a holy man. What if, when I am laid into the tomb, I wake before the time that Romeo comes to save me? There's a terrifying thought! Shall I not, then, be trapped in the vault, who's foul mouth breathes in no healthy air and there die suffocating before my Romeo comes? Or, if I live, is it not very likely the horrible fancies of death and night, together with the terror of the place, as can be expected in a vault, an ancient receptacle where for many hundred years the bones of all my buried ancestors are packed...

Where bloody Tybalt, yet but green in earth,
Lies festering in his shroud; where, as they say,
At some hours in the night spirits resort;
Alack, alack, is it not like that I,
So early waking, what with loathsome smells,
And shrieks like mandrakes' torn out of the earth,
That living mortals, hearing them, run mad?
O, if I wake, shall I not be distraught,
Environed with all these hideous fears?
And madly play with my forefather's joints?
And pluck the mangled Tybalt from his shroud?
And, in this rage, with some great kinsman's bone,
As with a club, dash out my desperate brains?
O, look! methinks I see my cousin's ghost
Seeking out Romeo, that did spit his body
Upon a rapier's point: stay, Tybalt, stay!
Romeo, Romeo, Romeo, I drink to thee.

[She drinketh off the vial falls upon her bed]

...where bloody Tybalt, yet recently buried, lies festering in his coffin; where, as they say, at some hours in the night spirits reside; Alas, alas, is it not likely that I, waking up early, what with despicable smells and shrieks like the (*mandrake : the plant most closely associated with living humans in most traditions around the world because it looks like a baby*) torn out of the earth, that when living mortals hear them, will turn mad (*so the legend goes*)? Oh, if I wake, shall I not be distraught, cornered by all these hideous fears? And like a mad person play with my forefather's bones? And take out the mangled Tybalt from his shroud? And in this rage, with some great ancestor's bone, like a club, bust out my desperate brains? Oh look! I think I see my cousin's ghost seeking out Romeo, who did spit his body upon a rapier's point (*like a hog-roast spit over a fire*): hold off, Tybalt, hold off! Romeo, Romeo, Romeo, I drink to you...

IV.IV

Main Hall in Capulet's Mansion.
Enter Lady Capulet and Nurse

Lady Capulet

Hold, take these keys and fetch more spices Nurse.

[*because spices were very rare and expensive they would be kept locked up in a safe place*]

Nurse

They call for dates and quinces in the pastry.

They need dates and [*quince : Asian kind of cooking apple*] in the bakers.

Enter Capulet

Capulet

Come, stir, stir, stir!
The second cock hath crow'd, the curfew-bell hath rung, 'tis three o'clock:
Look to the baked meats, good Angelica:
Spare not for the cost.

Come, move, move, move! The second cock has crowed, the curfew-bell has rung, it's three o'clock: check on the baked meats good Angelica [*Nurse's first name*]! Don't worry about how much anything costs.

Nurse

Go, you cot-quean, go, get you to bed; faith,
You'll be sick to-morrow for this night's watching.

Go, you [*cot-quean : a man who plays the part of a housewife, she is teasing him*] go, get you to bed; honestly, you'll be sick tomorrow because of this night's organisation.

Capulet

No, not a whit: what! I have watch'd ere now
All night for lesser cause and ne'er been sick.

No, no matter at all: what? I have stayed up all night before now for less important reasons and never been sick.

Lady Capulet

Ay, you have been a mouse-hunt in your time;
But I will watch you from such watching now.

[*Exeunt Lady Capulet and Nurse*]

Yes, you have been a [*mouse-hunt : weasel, 'womaniser'*] in your time but I will direct you from such a direction now [*as womanising*].

Capulet

A jealous hood, a jealous hood!

Equivalent to saying: What a mad woman, a mad woman [*in jest*]!

Enter three or four Servingmen,
w spits, logs and baskets

Now, fellow, What's there?

First Servant

Things for the cook, sir; but I know not what.

Capulet

Make haste, make haste.

[*Exit First Servant*]

Sirrah, fetch drier logs:
Call Peter, he will show thee where they are.

Sirrah, get some dry logs [*for the fire*]: call Peter, he will show where they are.

Second Servant

I have a head, sir, that will find out logs,
And never trouble Peter for the matter.

[*Exit Second Servant*]

I have a head, sir, that can find logs and never have to trouble Peter for the matter.

Capulet

Mass, and well said; a merry whoreson, ha!
Thou shalt be logger-head. Good faith, 'tis day:
The county will be here with music straight,
For so he said he would: I hear him near.

[*Music within*]

Nurse! Wife! What, ho! What, Nurse, I say!

Yesss and well said: a merry motherf****er, ha! I'll call you 'loghead'. Good faith, it is day: the count will be here with music soon for so he said he would: I hear him near.

Enter Nurse

84

Go waken Juliet, go and trim her up;
I'll go and chat with Paris: hie, make haste,
Make haste; the bridegroom he is come already:
                              Make haste, I say.
                                      Exeunt

Go and wake up Juliet, go and get her ready: I'll go and chat with Paris: go, and hurry up, hurry up, the bridegroom is already here: hurry up, I say.

I. V

                    Juliet's bed-chamber.
                       Enter Nurse
Nurse
          Mistress! what, mistress! Juliet! fast, I
warrant her, she- Why, lamb?! why, lady! fie, you
slug-a-bed! Why, love, I say! madam! sweet-heart!
why, bride! What, not a word? you take your
pennyworths now; Sleep for a week; for the next
night, I warrant, the County Paris hath set up his
rest, that you shall rest but little. God forgive me,
Marry, and amen, how sound is she asleep!
I must needs wake her. Madam, madam, madam!
Ay, let the county take you in your bed;
He'll fright you up, i' faith. Will it not be?

Mistress! What, mistress! Juliet! Fast asleep, I bet- why, lamb?! Why, lady! Damn you slug-of-the-bed! Why, love, I say! Madam! Sweet-heart! Why, bride! What, not a word? For now you just need a [*pennyworths : a little bit*] of sleep; you'll sleep for a week after tonight, I warrant, the Count Paris has [*set up his rest : a card game term meaning he has claimed such a large stake that he doesn't have to play for at least the next few hands*] so that you will have only a little rest [*because he will be shagging to you all night*]. God forgive me, by Mary and amen, how sound asleep she is! I must wake her up. Madam, madam, madam! Fine, let the count take you in your bed; he'll scare you awake, in faith. Will it not be so?

What, dress'd! and in your clothes! and down again!
I must needs wake you; Lady! lady! lady!
Alas, alas! Help, help! my lady's dead!
O, well-a-day, that ever I was born!
Some aqua vitae, ho! My lord! my lady!

What, dressed?! And in your clothes [*she didn't bother getting dressed for bed the night before*]? And now you'll have to undress again to put on the right ones? I must wake you up; Lady! Lady! Lady! Alas, alas! Help, help! My lady's dead! Oh, it were best I had never been born! Some whisky [*to wake Juliet up*]! My lord! My lady!

                       Enter Lady Capulet
Lady Capulet
          What noise is here?
Nurse
          O lamentable day!
Lady Capulet
          What is the matter?
Nurse
          Look, look! O heavy day!
Lady Capulet
          O me, O me! My child, my only life,
Revive, look up, or I will die with thee!
                    Help, help! Call help.

                       Enter Capulet
Capulet
          For shame, bring Juliet forth; her lord is come.
Nurse
          She's dead, deceased, she's dead; alack the day!
Lady Capulet
          Alack the day, she's dead, she's dead, she's dead!

85

Capulet

Ha! let me see her: out, alas! She's cold.
Her blood is settled and her joints are stiff;
Life and these lips have long been separated:
Death lies on her like an untimely frost
Upon the sweetest flower of all the field.

Nurse

O lamentable day!

Lady Capulet

O woeful time!

Capulet

Death, that hath ta'en her hence to make me wail,
Ties up my tongue, and will not let me speak.

Enter Friar Laurence and Paris w Musicians

Friar Laurence

Come, is the bride ready to go to church?

Capulet

Ready to go but never to return.
O son! the night before thy wedding-day
Hath Death lain with thy wife. There she lies,
Flower as she was, deflowered by him.
Death is my son-in-law, Death is my heir;
My daughter he hath wedded: I will die,
And leave him all; life, living, all is Death's.

Ready to go but never to return. Oh son [*to Paris*]! The night before your wedding-day has Death slept with your wife. There she lies, flower as she was, her virginity stolen by him. Death is my son-in-law, Death is my heir; my daughter he has wedded: I will die and leave him everything; life, living, all is Death's.

Paris

Have I thought long to see this morning's face,
And doth it give me such a sight as this?

I've been looking forward to this morning for a long time and now I am given such a sight as this?

Lady Capulet

Accursed, unhappy, wretched, hateful day!
Most miserable hour that e'er time saw
In lasting labour of his pilgrimage!
But one, poor one, one poor and loving child,
But one thing to rejoice and solace in,
And cruel Death hath catch'd it from my sight!

Cursed, terrible, wretched, hateful day! The most miserable hour that time ever saw in the everlasting labour of his pilgrimage [*time is like a monk travelling forever towards the end/heaven*]! But one, poor one, one poor and loving child, the one thing I had to rejoice and solace in and cruel Death has snatched it from my sight!

Nurse

O woe! O woeful, woeful, woeful day!
Most lamentable day, most woeful day,
That ever, ever, I did yet behold! O day! O day!
O day! O hateful day!
        Never was seen so black a day as this:
O woeful day, O woeful day!

Paris

Beguiled, divorced, wronged, spited, slain!
Most detestable Death, by thee beguil'd,
By cruel cruel thee quite overthrown!
O love! O life! not life, but love in death!

Deceived, divorced, wronged, spited, slain! Most detestable Death, by you deceived, by cruel cruel you quite overthrown! Oh love! Oh life! Not life [*because she is dead*] but love in Death!

Capulet

Despised, distressed, hated, martyr'd, kill'd!
Uncomfortable time, why camest thou now
To murder, murder our solemnity?
O child! O child! my soul, and not my child!

Despised, distressed, hated, martyred, killed! Comfort-less time, why come you now to murder, murder our ceremony? Oh child! Oh child! My soul and not my child [*this is touching, he is saying he would rather spend eternity in hell than*

Dead art thou! Alack! my child is dead;
And with my child my joys are buried.
Friar Laurence
    Peace, ho, for shame! confusion's cure lives not
In these confusions. Heaven and yourself
Had part in this fair maid; now heaven hath all,
And all the better is it for the maid:
Your part in her you could not keep from death,
But heaven keeps his part in eternal life.
The most you sought was her promotion;
For 'twas your heaven she should be advanced:
And weep ye now, seeing she is advanced
Above the clouds, as high as heaven itself?
O, in this love, you love your child so ill,
That you run mad, seeing that she is well:
She's not well married that lives married long;
But she's best married that dies married young.
Dry up your tears, and stick your rosemary
On this fair corse; and, as the custom is,
In all her best array bear her to church:
For though fond nature bids us all lament,
Yet nature's tears are reason's merriment.
Capulet
    All things that we ordained festival,
Turn from their office to black funeral;
Our instruments to melancholy bells,
Our wedding cheer to a sad burial feast,
Our solemn hymns to sullen dirges change,
Our bridal flowers serve for a buried corse,
And all things change them to the contrary.
Friar Laurence
    Sir, go you in; and, madam, go with him;
And go, Sir Paris; every one prepare
To follow this fair corse unto her grave:
The heavens do lour upon you for some ill;
Move them no more by crossing their high will.
            [Exeunt Capulet & Lady Capulet,
                    Paris and Friar Laurence]
First Musician
    Faith, we may put up our pipes and be gone.
Nurse
    Honest goodfellows, ah, put up, put up;
        For, well you know, this is a pitiful case.
            [Exit Nurse]

First Musician
    Ay, by my troth, the case may be amended.

        Enter Peter
Peter
    Musicians, O, musicians, 'Heart's ease,
Heart's ease:' O, an you will have me live, play
                'Heart's ease.'

let Juliet die)! Dead are you! Alas! My child is
dead and with my child my joys are buried.

Peace, for shame! Devastation's cure lives not in
these ramblings. Heaven and yourself both
shared this maid: now heaven has all and all the
better is it for the maid: your part in her you
could not keep from death but heaven keeps his
part in eternal life. The most you wanted for her
was to be married for it was your heaven that
she should be so: and now you weep, seeing she
is advanced above the clouds as high as heaven
itself? Oh, in this love, you love your child so badly
that you run mad seeing that she is well; she's
not well married that lives married long (because
people get sick of each other) but she's best
married that dies married young (so that one
only knows the pleasures of marriage). Dry up
your tears and stick your (rosemary : the flower
of remembrance) on this fair corpse and, as the
custom is, in all her best dress carry her to
church: for although our fond natures make us
want to cry, in nature tears are intellect's joy.

All things that we arranged for the festival turn
from their style into a black funeral; our
instruments to sad songs, our wedding cheer to
a sad burial feast, our solemn hymns change to
brooding mournings, our bridal flowers place
with the buried corpse and all things change
them to the opposite.

Sir, go you in, and madam, go with him; and go,
Sir Paris, everyone prepare to follow this fair
corpse to her grave; the heavens do scowl upon
you for some sin; don't upset them any more by
betraying their customs.

Indeed, we can put up our pipes and be gone.

Honest good-men, ah, put up, put up, for well you
know this is a sorrowful happening.

Yes, by my truth 1. things could be better 2.
unlike Juliet, the case for my instrument can be
mended if it is broken.

Musicians, oh, musicians, 'Heart's ease, Heart's
ease'. Oh, if you will have me live, play 'Heart's
ease' (a song).

87

First Musician

Why 'Heart's ease?'

Peter

O, musicians, because my heart itself plays 'My heart is full of woe:' O, play me some merry dump, to comfort me.

First Musician

Not a dump we; 'tis no time to play now.

Peter

You will not, then?

First Musician

No.

Peter

I will then give it you soundly.

First Musician

What will you give us?

Peter

No money, on my faith, but the gleek;
          I will give you the minstrel.

First Musician

Then I will give you the serving-creature.

Peter

Then will I lay the serving-creature's dagger on your pate. I will carry no crotchets: I'll re you, I'll fa you; do you note me?

First Musician

An you re us and fa us, you note us.

Second Musician

Pray you, put up your dagger, and put out your wit.

Peter

Then have at you with my wit! I will dry-beat you with an iron wit, and put up my iron dagger. Answer me like men:

[Singing]

'When griping grief the heart doth wound,
    And doleful dumps the mind oppress,
    Then music with her silver sound-'

-why 'silver sound'? why 'music with her silver sound'? What say you, Simon Catling?

Musician

Marry, sir, because silver hath a sweet sound.

Peter

Pretty! What say you, Hugh Rebec?

Second Musician

I say 'silver sound,' because musicians sound for silver.

Peter

Pretty too! What say you, James Soundpost?

Why Heart's ease?

Oh musicians, because my heart itself plays 'My heart is full of woe': O, play me some merry [*dump : a sad song*] to comfort me.

We'll not play a dump, us; this is no time to play now.

I give it to you straight then.

No money, on my faith, but a taunt: You're nothing more than a [*minstrel : wandering musicians, renowned for being liars, thieves and cheats*].

Then I can tell you are nothing more than a lowly servant.

Then I will put the lowly servant's dagger to your jaw. 1. I'll not sing no notes 2. I'll not endure your insults: I'll make you sing high, I'll make you sing low – do you take note of me?

If you make us sing high and low, you note us.

Pray you, put up your dagger and stop showing off.

Then have at you with my wit! I will [*dry-beat : beat with a sword without drawing blood*] you with an iron wit and put away my iron dagger. Answer me like men:

*'When gripping onto grief the heart does wound
and mournful sad-songs the mind oppress
then music with her silver sound -'*

-why 'silver sound'? Why 'music with her silver sound'? What say you, Simon [*catling : a musical string made from cat gut*]?

Truly, sir, because the word 'silver' sounds sweet.

Good answer! What say you, Hugh [*rebec : a fiddle with three-strings*]?

I say 'silver sound' because musicians make sound for silver.
                    Another good answer!
What say you, James [*soundpost : the vibrating spine that joins guitars, violins etc.*]?

88

Third Musician

    Faith, I know not what to say.

Peter

    O, I cry you mercy; you are the singer: I will say for you. It is 'music with her silver sound,' because musicians have no gold for sounding: 'Then music with her silver sound With speedy help doth lend redress.'

                           [Exit Peter]

Oh, I beg your pardon; you are the singer; I will say for you. It is *'music with her silver sound'* because musicians have no gold for making sound: *'then music with her silver sound with speedy help does lend comfort* [i.e. because they cannot get paid in gold they must cheer themselves up with music]*'*.

First Musician

    What a pestilent knave is this same!

What an irritating [*knave : similar to Sirrah, but more derogatory, in fact, downright rude*]

Second Musician

    Hang him, Jack! Come, we'll in here; tarry for the mourners, and stay dinner.

                      Exeunt

Forget about him, Jack! Come, we'll go in here, wait for the mourners and stay for dinner.

89

<u>Commentary : Act IV</u>

Act IV is Juliet's act. Running into Paris at the church? Disgusting. What does he say to her? *"Thou face is mine,"* What a creep. Anyway, it seems Juliet and Romeo are a good match because no sooner than Juliet arrives in Friar Laurence's cell before she too is seriously inclined to commit suicide rather than live in a world without her first love. I suppose the most obvious question that should be asked at this point is; just how stupid is the Friar, really? Looking back 'with the benefit of hindsight' it is easy to shake our heads in disbelief at how utterly foolish the idea was, but perhaps, as Friar Laurence says at the time *"[The solution] craves as desperate an action as that which we would like to prevent."* Listening to the Friar explain his plan, it is as though he is casting a spell, describing the effects of the poison in chronological stages as we picture the integral event unfolding in our minds outside of the narrative we get to see portrayed on stage. All this is said as he produces the poison in question and like the Friar and Juliet themselves, we cannot help but stare upon it in menacing wonder. Picture it; 1500 in the audience of the Globe theatre, one holy Friar and one desperate Juliet, every one of them focused intently on that one little vial of potion. I repeat; as the Friar talks us through the process, it is as though he is casting a spell over the entire plot, holding that vial up like a magic wand. In this way, because of the supernatural notions we associate with the effects of the drug, and particularly when we witness the iconic finale it all results in, we are left feeling that perhaps the Friar wasn't so pathetically stupid after all, that perhaps he was just a device, just another fish in the currents of destiny that have been conspiring to bring about this detestable fortune.

Watching the Capulets prepare for Juliet's wedding is appalling. They busy themselves away, blissfully unaware of the imminent disaster. Once in her chamber, just as instructed, Juliet sends the Nurse away then has one more chance to contemplate her life before plunging into paralysis for a full 42 hours. This is her only way out, it's time to make it or break it. Full of desperation and terror her youthful imagination runs wild and she shakes with fear to contemplate the monstrous setting she will awake to. She envisions suffocating and going insane and bashing her own brains out but little does Juliet know that the reality she will in fact awake to is more terrible than any of her imaginings.

"Romeo, Romeo, Romeo, I drink to thee."

ACT V

Mantua. A street. Enter Romeo

Romeo

If I may trust the flattering truth of sleep,
My dreams presage some joyful news at hand:
My bosom's lord sits lightly in his throne;
And all this day an unaccustom'd spirit
Lifts me above the ground with cheerful thoughts.
I dreamt my lady came and found me dead -
Strange dream, that gives a dead man leave
to think! - And breathed such life with kisses in my
lips, that I revived, and was an emperor.
Ah me! how sweet is love itself possess'd,
When but love's shadows are so rich in joy!

Mantua is the town where Romeo is hiding out.

If I can trust the nice things I am told when asleep, my dreams predict some good news is coming any second: my bosom's lord (*heart*) sits happily in his throne (*the chest*) and all day an unusual spirit has lifted me above the ground with cheerful thoughts. I dreamt my lady (*Juliet*) came and found me dead – a strange dream that gives a dead man permission to think! - and breathed such life with kisses in my lips, that I came back to life and was an emperor. Ah me! How sweet is love when actually possessed, considering that love's shadows are so rich in joy!

Enter Balthasar on horseback
News from Verona! How now, Balthasar!
Dost thou not bring me letters from the friar?
How doth my lady? Is my father well?
How fares my Juliet? that I ask again;
For nothing can be ill, if she be well.

Balthasar

Then she is well, and nothing can be ill:
Her body sleeps in Capel's monument,
And her immortal part with angels lives.
I saw her laid low in her kindred's vault,
And presently took post to tell it you:
O, pardon me for bringing these ill news,
Since you did leave it for my office, sir.

Then she is well and nothing can be wrong: her body sleeps in the Capulet's burial chamber and her immortal soul lives with the angels. I saw her laid down in her family's crypt and immediately came to tell you of this news. Oh forgive me for delivering this terrible news, because you left that task to me (*of bringing any news from Verona*), sir.

Romeo

Is it even so? then I defy you, stars!
Thou know'st my lodging: get me ink and paper,
And hire post-horses; I will hence to-night.

Is it even so? Then I defy you, stars! You know where I live: get me ink and paper and hire post-horses (*horses for delivering mail, fast and with high stamina*); I will go from here tonight.

Balthasar

I do beseech you, sir, have patience:
Your looks are pale and wild, and do import
Some misadventure.

I do beg you, sir, be patient: you look pale and wild and do seem like you mean to do some craziness.

Romeo

Tush, thou art deceived:
Leave me, and do the thing I bid thee do.
Hast thou no letters to me from the friar?

Tush, you are mistaken: leave me and do the thing I asked you to. Have you no letters to me from the friar?

Balthasar

No, my good lord.

Romeo

No matter: get thee gone,
And hire those horses; I'll be with thee straight.
[Exit Balthasar]
Well, Juliet, I will lie with thee to-night.
Let's see for means: O mischief, thou art swift
To enter in the thoughts of desperate men!
I do remember an Apothecary,
- And hereabouts he dwells - which late I noted

Well, Juliet, I will lie with you tonight. Let's see how we can do this: oh, mischief, you are swift to enter the thoughts of desperate men! I do remember an (*Apothecary : chemist*) – and he lives around here – who lately I noticed was

91

In tatter'd weeds, with overwhelming brows,
Culling of simples; meagre were his looks,
Sharp misery had worn him to the bones:
And in his needy shop a tortoise hung,
An alligator stuff'd, and other skins
Of ill-shaped fishes; and about his shelves
A beggarly account of empty boxes,
Green earthen pots, bladders and musty seeds,
Remnants of packthread and old cakes of roses,
Were thinly scatter'd, to make up a show.
Noting this penury, to myself I said
'An if a man did need a poison now,
Whose sale is present death in Mantua,
Here lives a caitiff wretch would sell it him.'
O, this same thought did but forerun my need;
And this same needy man must sell it me.
As I remember, this should be the house.
Being holiday, the beggar's shop is shut.
What, ho! Apothecary!

wearing tattered clothes and had dark eyes, who was gathering (*simples : medicinal plants*): he looked small and weak, as though painful misery had worn him to the bones: and in his shop that needs more customers a tortoise hung, there was a stuffed alligator and other skins of sinister fishes and about his shelves a petty assortment of empty boxes, unfired clay pots, bladders and musky seeds, pieces of packaging string and old crushed roses, were thinly scattered across the shelf to make a display. Noting this poverty, I said to myself 'and if a man did need a poison now, whose sale is punishable by death in Mantua, here lives a miserable wretch who would sell it to him.' Oh, this same thought did foreshadow my need; and this same needy man must sell it to me. As I remember, this should be the house. Being a holiday, the beggar's shop is shut. Hey, YO! Apothecary!

Enter Apothecary

Apothecary
Who calls so loud?

Romeo
Come hither, man. I see that thou art poor:
Hold, there is forty ducats: let me have
A dram of poison, such soon-speeding gear
As will disperse itself through all the veins
That the life-weary taker may fall dead
And that the trunk may be discharged of breath
As violently as hasty powder fired
Doth hurry from the fatal cannon's womb.

Come here man. I see that you are poor. Hold this, there is forty (*ducats : gold pieces*): let me have a drop of poison, gear that works so quickly that it will disperse itself through all the veins and so that the (*life-weary : depressed*) taker will fall dead and that the body will be expelled of breath as violently as gun powder fired does hurry from the fatal cannon's womb (*barrel*).

Apothecary
Such mortal drugs I have; but Mantua's law
Is death to any he that utters them.

I have such lethal drugs: but Mantua's law is death to any person that even speaks of them.

Romeo
Art thou so bare and full of wretchedness,
And fear'st to die? famine is in thy cheeks,
Need and oppression starveth in thine eyes,
Contempt and beggary hangs upon thy back;
The world is not thy friend nor the world's law;
The world affords no law to make thee rich;
Then be not poor, but break it, and take this.
[*Handing him the gold*]

Are you so poorly and full of wretchedness and yet you are afraid to die? Famine is in your cheeks, need and distress starving in your eyes, scorn and poverty hangs upon your back; the world is not your friend nor is the world's law; the world has no law to make you rich; then stop being poor by breaking it and take this.

Apothecary
My poverty, but not my will, consents.

My poverty but not my will agrees.

Romeo
I pay thy poverty and not thy will.

I pay your poverty and not your will.

Apothecary
Put this in any liquid thing you will,
And drink it off; and, if you had the strength
Of twenty men, it would dispatch you straight.

Mix this with any other liquid you like and drink it off and if you had the strength of twenty men it would still kill you straight away.

Romeo

There is thy gold, worse poison to men's souls,
Doing more murders in this loathsome world,
Than these poor compounds that thou mayst not sell.
I sell thee poison; thou hast sold me none.
Farewell: buy food, and get thyself in flesh.
Come, cordial and not poison, go with me
To Juliet's grave; for there must I use thee.

Exeunt

There is your gold, which is a much worse poison to men's souls, doing more murders in this terrible world than these cheap chemicals that you are not allowed to sell. I sell you poison; you have sold me none. Goodbye; buy food and put on some weight. Come, cordial (*Ribena or orange squash is a cordial as they are supposed to be mixed first, just like the poison*) and not poison, go with me to Juliet's grave for there must I use you.

There is thy gold, worse poison to men's souls, Doing more murder in this loathsome world Than these poor compounds that thou mayst not sell.

I.VV

Friar Laurence's cell.
Enter Friar John

Friar John

Holy Franciscan friar! brother, ho!

Enter Friar Laurence

Friar Laurence

This same should be the voice of Friar John.
Welcome from Mantua: what says Romeo?
Or, if his mind be writ, give me his letter.

I'd know that voice, it's Friar John! Welcome back from Mantua, what did Romeo say? Or, if he wrote his thoughts down, give me his letter.

Friar John

Going to find a bare-foot brother out
One of our order, to associate me,
Here in this city visiting the sick,
And finding him, the searchers of the town,
Suspecting that we both were in a house
Where the infectious pestilence did reign,
Seal'd up the doors, and would not let us forth;
So that my speed to Mantua there was stay'd.

Going to find a (*bare-foot : friars often travelled bare-foot or at best in sandals*) brother (*another friar*) to accompany me (*because friars always travel in pairs*), he was somewhere in the city visiting the sick and when I found him the health-police of the town, suspecting that because we were both in a house where the infected live, sealed up the doors and would not let us go; so it was that my journey to Mantua stayed right there.

Friar Laurence

Who bore my letter, then, to Romeo?

Friar John

I could not send it - here it is again -
Nor get a messenger to bring it thee,
So fearful were they of infection.

I could not send it – here it is again – nor could I find a messenger to bring it to you so scared they were of getting infected.

Friar Laurence

Unhappy fortune! by my brotherhood,
The letter was not nice but full of charge
Of dear import, and the neglecting it
May do much danger. Friar John, go hence;
Get me an iron crow, and bring it straight
Unto my cell.

Unhappy fortune! By my brotherhood, the letter was not a nice little message but full of directions of dear importance and the neglecting of it may do much danger. Friar John, go from here: get me an iron crow-bar and bring it straight to my room.

Friar John

Brother, I'll go and bring it thee.

[*Exit Friar John*]

Friar Laurence

Now must I to the monument alone;
Within three hours will fair Juliet wake:
She will beshrew me much that Romeo
Hath had no notice of these accidents;
But I will write again to Mantua,
And keep her at my cell till Romeo come;
Poor living corse, closed in a dead man's tomb!

Now I must go to the graveyard alone; within three hours the fair Juliet will wake up; she will curse me that Romeo has no knowledge of these accidents; but I will write again to Mantua and keep her at my cell until Romeo comes; poor living corpse, closed in a dead man's tomb!

Exit

I.VVV

The Churchyard;
The Tomb of the Capulets.
Enter Paris and his Page
bearing flowers & a torch

Paris

> Give me thy torch, boy: hence, and stand aloof-
> Yet put it out, for I would not be seen.
> Under yond yew-trees lay thee all along,
> Holding thine ear close to the hollow ground;
> So shall no foot upon the churchyard tread,
> Being loose, unfirm, with digging up of graves,
> But thou shalt hear it: whistle then to me,
> As signal that thou hear'st something approach.
> Give me those flowers. Do as I bid thee, go.

Give me your torch, boy: go over there and stand at a distance – actually, put it out (*the torch*), for I do not want to be seen. Under those yew-trees hang around all along there, holding your ear close to the hollow ground so that no foot can tread upon the churchyard, being loose and not firm what with the digging up of graves, without you hearing it: then whistle to me as a signal that you hear someone approaching. Give me those flowers. Do as I told you, go.

Page [Aside]

> I am almost afraid to stand alone
> Here in the churchyard; yet I will adventure.
>
> [Exit Page]

Paris

> Sweet flower, with flowers thy bridal bed I
> strew - O woe! thy canopy is dust and stones -
> Which with sweet water nightly I will dew,
> Or, wanting that, with tears distill'd by moans:
> The obsequies that I for thee will keep
> Nightly shall be to strew thy grave and weep.
>
> [The Page whistles]
>
> The boy gives warning something doth approach.
> What cursed foot wanders this way to-night,
> To cross my obsequies and true love's rite?
> What with a torch! muffle me, night, awhile.
>
> [Paris retires]

Sweet flower (*Juliet*), I scatter your bridal bed with flowers – Oh sorrow! Your tomb is dust and stones – which with sweet water I will sprinkle nightly or, failing that, (*instead of sweet water*) with tears distilled by moans: the rites of the dead that I for you will keep nightly shall be to scatter your grave with flowers and weep.

The boy gives me warning something does approach. What cursed foot wanders this way tonight to cross my rites of the dead and true love's ritual? What, with a torch? Hide me, night, for awhile...

Enter Romeo and Balthasar,
w torch, mattock & iron crow

Romeo

> Give me that mattock and the wrenching iron.
> Hold, take this letter; early in the morning
> See thou deliver it to my lord and father.
> Give me the light: upon thy life, I charge thee,
> Whate'er thou hear'st or seest, stand all aloof,
> And do not interrupt me in my course.
> Why I descend into this bed of death,
> Is partly to behold my lady's face;
> But chiefly to take thence from her dead finger
> A precious ring, a ring that I must use
> In dear employment: therefore hence, be gone:
> But if thou, jealous, dost return to pry
> In what I further shall intend to do,
> By heaven, I will tear thee joint by joint
> And strew this hungry churchyard with thy limbs:

Give me that spade and the crowbar. Wait, take this letter; early in the morning see that you deliver it to my lord and father. Give me the light: upon your life, I charge you, whatever you hear or see, stand at a distance and do not interrupt me in my actions. The reason I descend into this bed of death is partly to see my lady's face but chiefly to take from her dead finger a precious ring, a ring that I must use for a very important matter (*Romeo is lying to get some privacy*): therefore, scram, be gone: but if you, feeling jealous, return to spy on what else I intend to do, by heaven, I will tear you limb from limb and scatter this hungry churchyard with your body parts.

The time and my intents are savage-wild,
More fierce and more inexorable far
Than empty tigers or the roaring sea.

Balthasar

    I will be gone, sir, and not trouble you.

Romeo

    So shalt thou show me friendship.
                Take thou that:
  Live, and be prosperous: and farewell, good fellow.

Balthasar [Aside]

    For all this same, I'll hide me hereabout:
        his looks I fear and his intents I doubt.

                      [Balthasar retires]

Romeo

    Thou detestable maw, thou womb of death,
Gorged with the dearest morsel of the earth,
Thus I enforce thy rotten jaws to open,
And, in despite, I'll cram thee with more food!
        [Breaking open the entrance to the tomb]

Paris [Aside]

    This is that banish'd haughty Montague,
That murder'd my love's cousin, with which grief,
It is supposed, the fair creature died;
And here is come to do some villainous shame
To the dead bodies: I will apprehend him.
        [Stepping forth and drawing his sword]
Stop thy unhallow'd toil, vile Montague!
Can vengeance be pursued further than death?
Condemned villain, I do apprehend thee:
Obey, and go with me; for thou must die.

Romeo

    I must indeed; and therefore came I hither.
Good gentle youth, tempt not a desperate man;
Fly hence, and leave me: think upon these gone;
Let them affright thee. I beseech thee, youth,
Put not another sin upon my head,
By urging me to fury: O, be gone!
By heaven, I love thee better than myself;
For I come hither arm'd against myself:
Stay not, be gone; live, and hereafter say,
A madman's mercy bade thee run away.

Paris

           I do defy thy conjurations,
And apprehend thee for a felon here.

Romeo [Drawing his sword]

    Wilt thou provoke me? then have at thee, boy!

        They engage & fight

Page

    O Lord, they fight! I will go call the watch.
                    [Exit Page]

The time and my intentions are savage and wild,
more fierce and far more unstoppable than
hungry tigers or the roaring sea.

In doing so, you show me friendship. Take that
[*the letter*]: live and do well for yourself and
farewell, good fellow.

Despite what he says, I'll hide myself hereabouts:
his looks, I fear and his intents I doubt.

You detestable jaws, you womb of death,
feasting on the dearest morsel of the earth
[*Juliet*], so it is I force your rotten jaws to open
and, to spite you, I'll cram you with more food
[*Romeo's body*]!

This is that banished arrogant Montague, that
murdered my love's cousin, by the grief of which,
it is supposed, the fair creature died; and here is
he come to do some villainous shame to the
dead bodies: I will apprehend him.

Stop your blasphemous actions, vile Montague!
Can vengeance be pursued further than death?
Condemned villain, I do arrest you: obey and go
with me for you must die.

I must indeed and that is why I have come. Good
gentle youth, tempt not a desperate man; run
from here and leave me: think about these dead
bodies around us, let them scare you. I beg of
you, youth, put not another sin upon my head by
urging me to fury: oh, be gone! By heaven, I love
you better than myself, for I come here armed
against myself: don't stay, just go, live and
hereafter say a madman's mercy asked you to
run away.

I do defy your [*conjurations : Paris fears Romeo
is intent on using black magic within the tomb*]
and apprehend you for being a felon.

Will you provoke me? Then have at you, boy!

Romeo succeeds in slaying Paris,
spilling his blood across the tomb entrance

Paris

　　O, I am slain!

[Paris falls hard]
　　If thou be merciful,
　　Open the tomb, lay me with Juliet.
[Paris dies]

Romeo

　　In faith, I will. Let me peruse this face.
Mercutio's kinsman, noble County Paris!
What said my man, when my betossed soul
Did not attend him as we rode? I think
He told me Paris should have married Juliet:
Said he not so? or did I dream it so?
Or am I mad, hearing him talk of Juliet,
To think it was so? O, give me thy hand,
One writ with me in sour misfortune's book!
I'll bury thee in a triumphant grave;
A grave? O no! a lantern, slaughter'd youth,
For here lies Juliet, and her beauty makes
This vault a feasting presence full of light.
Death, lie thou there, by a dead man interr'd.
[Laying Paris in the monument]
How oft when men are at the point of death
Have they been merry! which their keepers call
A lightning before death:
[Upon discovering Juliet's body] O, how may I
Call this a lightning? O my love! My wife!
Death, that hath suck'd the honey of thy breath,
Hath had no power yet upon thy beauty:
Thou art not conquer'd; beauty's ensign yet
Is crimson in thy lips and in thy cheeks,
And death's pale flag is not advanced there.
Tybalt, liest thou there in thy bloody sheet?
O, what more favour can I do to thee,
Than with that hand that cut thy youth in twain
To sunder his that was thine enemy?
Forgive me, cousin! Ah, dear Juliet,
Why art thou yet so fair? shall I believe
That unsubstantial death is amorous,
And that the lean abhorred monster keeps
Thee here in dark to be his paramour?
For fear of that, I still will stay with thee;
And never from this palace of dim night
Depart again: here, here will I remain
With worms that are thy chamber-maids; O, here
Will I set up my everlasting rest,
And shake the yoke of inauspicious stars
From this world-wearied flesh. Eyes, look your last!
Arms, take your last embrace! And, lips, O you
The doors of breath, seal with a righteous kiss

In faith, I will. Let me get a good look at his face...
Mercutio's family, noble Count Paris! What was
it my man (*Balthasar*) said, when my mixed-up
soul was not paying attention as we rode [back
to Verona]? I think he told me Paris was the one
who was going to marry Juliet: said he not so?
Or did I dream it so? Or am I mad, hearing him
talk of Juliet to think it was so? Oh, give me your
hand, you have been written with me in sour
misfortune's book! I'll bury you in a triumphant
grave; a grave? Oh no! More like a (*lantern : a
very well lit hall such as churches are and at
parties*), slaughtered youth, for here lies Juliet
and her beauty makes this tomb a feasting hall
full of light. Death (*Paris*), you lie there, laid to
rest by a dead man (*Romeo*).

How often when men are at the point of death,
they have been merry! Which their nurses call a
lightning before death: oh, how may I call this a
lightning? Oh my love! My wife! Death, that has
sucked the honey of your breath, has had no
power yet upon your beauty: you are not
conquered: beauty's banner is still crimson in
your lips and in your cheeks and death's pale
standard has not advanced there. Tybalt, you lie
there in your bloody sheet? Oh, what better
favour can I do for you, than with that hand that
cut your youth in two, to break-apart his that was
your enemy (*Romeo*)? Forgive me, cousin! Ah,
dear Juliet, why are you still so beautiful? Shall I
believe that flimsy death is in love with you and
that the lean horrible monster keeps you here in
the dark to be his lover?

For fear of that, I will stay with you forever and
never depart from this palace of dim night: here,
here will I remain with worms that are your
chambermaids: oh, here will I set up my
everlasting rest and shake off the genesis of
unfavourable stars from this flesh tired of the
world. Eyes, look your last! Arms, take your last
embrace! And lips, oh you the doors of breath,
seal with a righteous kiss

A dateless bargain to engrossing death!
Come, bitter conduct, come, unsavoury guide!
Thou desperate pilot, now at once run on
The dashing rocks thy sea-sick weary bark!
Here's to my love!
                [Romeo drinks off the poison]
O true apothecary! Thy drugs are quick.
            Thus with a kiss I die.
          [Romeo kisses his love, then dies]

           Enter Friar Laurence
       at the other end of the churchyard,
        w a lantern, crow, and spade

Friar Laurence
    Saint Francis be my speed! how oft to-night
  Have my old feet stumbled at graves! Who's there?
Balthasar
    Here's one, a friend, and one that knows you well.
Friar Laurence
    Bliss be upon you! Tell me, good my friend,
What torch is yond, that vainly lends his light
To grubs and eyeless skulls? as I discern,
It burneth in the Capel's monument.
Balthasar
    It doth so, holy sir; and there's my master,
                  One that you love.
Friar Laurence
    Who is it?
Balthasar
    Romeo.
Friar Laurence
    How long hath he been there?
Balthasar
    Full half an hour.
Friar Laurence
    Go with me to the vault.
Balthasar
    I dare not, sir my master knows not but I am
gone hence; and fearfully did menace me with death,
If I did stay to look on his intents.
Friar Laurence
    Stay, then; I'll go alone. Fear comes upon me:
O, much I fear some ill unlucky thing.
Balthasar
    As I did sleep under this yew-tree here,
I dreamt my master and another fought,
And that my master slew him.
Friar Laurence
    Romeo!
               [Friar Laurence advances]
Alack, alack, what blood is this, which stains
The stony entrance of this sepulchre?

---

an eternal contract with all-absorbing death!
Come, bitter guide, come, vulgar path!
You desperate pilot [*the person who steers a
ship is the pilot*], now at once run onto the
shattering rocks your sea-sick, tired bark [*crash
the ship deliberately*]! Here's to my love!

Saint Francis help me speed! How often tonight
have my old feet stumbled over graves! Who's
there?

Only one person, a friend and one that knows you
well.

Bliss be upon you! Tell me, truthfully my friend,
what torch is over there that pointlessly lends
his light to grubs and eyeless skulls? As I can tell,
it burns in the Capulet's monument.

It does, holy sir and there is my master, one that
you love.

I dare not, sir, my master doesn't know but
thinks I am gone from here and seriously did he
threaten me with death if I did stay to look upon
what he intends to do.

[*perhaps he is lying because he does not want to
be in trouble for not breaking them up however
it is known that in states of great fear one
perceives reality as though in a dream*]

Alas, alas, what blood is this, which stains the
stony entrance of this tomb?

What mean these masterless and gory swords
To lie discolour'd by this place of peace?
                              [Enters the monument]
Romeo! O, pale! Who else? what, Paris too?
And steep'd in blood? Ah, what an unkind hour
Is guilty of this lamentable chance!
                              The lady stirs.

What means these [masterless : the swords
are left on the ground by themselves i.e. they
have no master] and gory swords that lie
coloured [red] in this place of peace? Romeo!
Oh pale! Who else? What, Paris too? And
steeped in blood? Ah, what unkind hour is guilty
of this cruel twist of fate? The lady stirs.

                    Juliet wakes
Juliet
    O comfortable friar! where is my lord?
I do remember well where I should be,
And there I am. Where is my Romeo?
                              [Noise within]

Oh comforting friar! Where is my lord? I do
remember well where I should be and here I am.
Where is my Romeo?

Friar Laurence
    I hear some noise. Lady, come from that nest
Of death, contagion, and unnatural sleep:
A greater power than we can contradict
Hath thwarted our intents. Come, come away.
Thy husband in thy bosom there lies dead;
And Paris too. Come, I'll dispose of thee
Among a sisterhood of holy nuns:
Stay not to question, for the watch is coming;
Come, go, good Juliet,
                              [Noise again]
I dare no longer stay.

I hear some noise. Lady, come from that nest of
death, sickness and unnatural sleep: a greater
power than we can oppose has defeated our
plan. Come, come away. Your husband in your
bosom there lies dead; and Paris too. Come, I'll
get rid of you by sending you to a sisterhood of
holy nuns: stay not to question for the night-
watch is coming; come, go, good Juliet.

Juliet
    Go, get thee hence, for I will not away.
                              [Exit Friar Laurence]
What's here? a cup, closed in my true love's hand?
Poison, I see, hath been his timeless end:
O churl! drunk all, and left no friendly drop
To help me after? I will kiss thy lips;
Haply some poison yet doth hang on them,
To make die with a restorative.
                              [Juliet kisses Romeo]
Thy lips are warm.

Go, get you from here, I will not leave.

What's here? A cup, closed in my true love's
hand? Poison, I see, has been his timeless end:
Oh you selfish person! You drunk it all and left no
friendly drop to help me after? I will kiss your lips,
perhaps some poison does still hang on them to
make me die with your medicine.

Your lips are warm.

First Watchman [Within]
    Lead, boy: which way?
Juliet
    Yea, noise? then I'll be brief. O happy dagger!
                              [Taking up Romeo's dagger]
This is thy sheath;
                              [Stabbing herself through]
there rust, and let me die.
    [Falling on Romeo's body, Juliet dies weeping]

Is that noise [is someone coming]? Then I will be
brief. Oh happy dagger! This [my body] is your
sheath [the case a blade is kept in]; there rust
and let me die.

        Enter Watch w the Page of Paris
Page
    This is the place; there, where the torch doth burn.

First Watchman

The ground is bloody; search about the
churchyard: Go, some of you, whoe'er you find
attach. Pitiful sight! here lies the county slain,
And Juliet bleeding, warm, and newly dead,
Who here hath lain these two days buried.
Go, tell the Prince: run to the Capulets:
Raise up the Montagues: some others search:
We see the ground whereon these woes do lie;
But the true ground of all these piteous woes
We cannot without circumstance descry.

The ground is bloody; search about the churchyard: go, some of you, arrest whoever you find. Pitiful sight! Here lies the count (*Paris*) slain and Juliet bleeding, warm and newly dead who has been lying here these past two days, buried. Go, tell the Prince: run to the Capulets: Wake up the Montagues: send some others to search more: we see the ground where these sorrows lie but the true reason of all these pitiful sorrows we cannot tell without the details.

Enter others of the Watch w Balthasar

Second Watchman

Here's Romeo's man; we found him in the
churchyard.

First Watchman

Hold him in safety, till the Prince come hither.

Enter others of the Watch w Friar Laurence

Third Watchman

Here is a friar, that trembles, sighs and weeps:
We took this mattock and this spade from him,
As he was coming from this churchyard side.

First Watchman

A great suspicion: stay the friar too.

Here is a friar who trembles and sighs and weeps: we took his spades from him as he was coming from this side of the churchyard.

How very suspicious: hold onto the friar too.

Enter the Prince & Attendants

Prince

What misadventure is so early up,
That calls our person from our morning's rest?

What misfortune is so early in the morning that calls me from my morning's rest?

Enter Capulet & Lady Capulet w others

Capulet

What should it be, that they so shriek abroad?

What is it that they scream about all around?

Lady Capulet

The people in the street cry Romeo,
Some Juliet, and some Paris; and all run,
With open outcry toward our monument.

The people in the street cry Romeo, some Juliet and some Paris; and all run openly shouting towards our family tomb.

Prince

What fear is this which startles in our ears?

What fear is this which startles our ears?

First Watchman

Sovereign, here lies the County Paris slain;
And Romeo dead; and Juliet, dead before,
Warm and new kill'd.

Sovereign, here lies the Count Paris slain; and Romeo dead and Juliet, dead before, warm and newly killed.

Prince

Search, seek, and know how this foul murder comes.

Search, seek and know how this foul murder came to pass.

First Watchman

Here is a friar, and slaughter'd Romeo's man;
With instruments upon them, fit to open
These dead men's tombs.

Here is a friar and slaughtered Romeo's friend; with instruments upon them, fit to open these dead men's tombs.

Capulet

    O heavens! O wife, look how our daughter
bleeds! This dagger hath mista'en - for, lo, his house
Is empty on the back of Montague -
And it mis-sheathed in my daughter's bosom!

Lady Capulet

    O me! this sight of death is as a bell,
That warns my old age to a sepulchre.

        Enter Montague and others

Prince

    Come, Montague; for thou art early up,
To see thy son and heir more early down.

Montague

    Alas, my liege, my wife is dead to-night;
Grief of my son's exile hath stopp'd her breath:
What further woe conspires against mine age?

Prince

    Look, and thou shalt see.

Montague

    O thou untaught! what manners is in this?
To press before thy father to a grave?

Prince

    Seal up the mouth of outrage for a while,
Till we can clear these ambiguities,
And know their spring, their head, their
true descent; and then will I be general of your woes,
And lead you even to death: meantime forbear,
And let mischance be slave to patience.
Bring forth the parties of suspicion.

Friar Laurence

    I am the greatest, able to do least,
Yet most suspected, as the time and place
Doth make against me of this direful murder;
And here I stand, both to impeach and purge
Myself condemned and myself excused.

Prince

    Then say at once what thou dost know in this.

Friar Laurence

    I will be brief, for my short date of breath
Is not so long as is a tedious tale.
Romeo, there dead, was husband to that Juliet;
And she, there dead, that Romeo's faithful wife:
I married them; and their stol'n marriage-day
Was Tybalt's dooms-day, whose untimely death
Banish'd the new-made bridegroom from the city,
For whom, and not for Tybalt, Juliet pined.
You, to remove that siege of grief from her,

Oh heavens! Oh wife, look how our daughter bleeds! This dagger is mistaken – for, look, his house is empty on the back of Montague (*presumably this means the dagger was held on a scabbard slung over Romeo's back. Surely this would mean Juliet found the dagger when embracing Romeo, with her arms wrapped around him*) - and is mis-sheathed in my daughter's bosom!

Oh me! This sight of death is as a bell that warns my old age that I am soon to be in a grave.

Come, Montague, for you are up early to see your son and heir killed ahead of his time.

Alas, my liege, my wife has also died tonight; grief of my son's exile has stopped her breath: what further sorrows conspire against my age?

Look and you shall see.

Oh you rude boy (*Romeo*)! What kind of manners is this? To rush before your father to your grave?

Seal up the door of this outrage for a while (*close the door of the crypt*) until we can clear these mysteries up and know how they started, what their minds were and how it all went down; and then I will be the leader of your sorrows and lead you even until death (*execute you if necessary?*): in the meantime, hold on and let this upset be slave to patience. Bring forward the suspicious parties.

I am the most suspect and the least able to excuse myself, as the time and place do connect me to this terrible murder; and here I stand, ready to both condemn and purge myself of what I am condemned and must excuse myself for.

I will be brief, for the short time before I die is not as long as is a tediously-told tale. Romeo, dead there, was husband to that Juliet; and she, there dead, was Romeo's faithful wife: I married them; and their stolen marriage day was Tybalt's dooms-day, whose untimely death banished the new-made bridegroom from the city, for whom and not for Tybalt, Juliet mourned. You, to remove that siege of grief from her,

Betroth'd and would have married her perforce
To County Paris: then comes she to me,
And, with wild looks, bid me devise some mean
To rid her from this second marriage,
Or in my cell there would she kill herself.
Then gave I her, so tutor'd by my art,
A sleeping potion; which so took effect
As I intended, for it wrought on her
The form of death: meantime I writ to Romeo,
That he should hither come as this dire night,
To help to take her from her borrow'd grave,
Being the time the potion's force should cease.
But he which bore my letter, Friar John,
Was stay'd by accident, and yesternight
Return'd my letter back. Then all alone
At the prefixed hour of her waking,
Came I to take her from her kindred's vault;
Meaning to keep her closely at my cell,
Till I conveniently could send to Romeo:
But when I came, some minute ere the time
Of her awaking, here untimely lay
The noble Paris and true Romeo dead.
She wakes; and I entreated her come forth,
And bear this work of heaven with patience:
But then a noise did scare me from the tomb;
And she, too desperate, would not go with me,
But, as it seems, did violence on herself.
All this I know; and to the marriage
Her nurse is privy: and, if aught in this
Miscarried by my fault, let my old life
Be sacrificed, some hour before his time,
Unto the rigour of severest law.

Prince

  We still have known thee for a holy man.
Where's Romeo's man? what can he say in this?

Balthasar

  I brought my master news of Juliet's death;
And then in post he came from Mantua
To this same place, to this same monument.
This letter he early bid me give his father,
And threatened me with death, going in the vault,
I departed not and left him there.

Prince

  Give me the letter; I will look on it.
Where is the county's page, that raised the watch?
Sirrah, what made your master in this place?

Page

  He came with flowers to strew his lady's grave;
And bid me stand aloof, and so I did:
Anon comes one with light to ope the tomb;
And by and by my master drew on him;
And then I ran away to call the watch.

promised her in marriage and would have married her by force to Count Paris: then she came to me, and, with wild looks, begged me to devise some means to rid her from this second marriage or in my cell there and then she would kill herself. So I gave in and tutored her about my skill [*as a herbologist*], a sleeping potion which took effect as I intended for it, seized her in the form of death: meanwhile, I wrote to Romeo that he should come here by tonight to help take her from her borrowed grave, it being the time when the potion's effect should end. But he who was carrying my letter, Friar John, was held up by accident and last night returned my letter back. Then all alone at the pre-determined hour of her waking, I came to take her from her family's crypt: meaning to keep her hidden in my cell until I could conveniently send for Romeo: but when I arrived, some minute before the time of her awaking, here untimely lay the noble Paris and true Romeo dead. She wakes and I begged her to come with me and bear this trick of heaven with patience: but then a noise did scare me away from the tomb and she, too desperate, would not go with me, but, as it seems, did violence on herself. All this I know and to the marriage her nurse is privy and if any of this is judged my fault then let my old life be sacrificed some hour before it's natural time, under the regulations of strictest law.

We still know you are a holy man. Where's Romeo's man? What can he say in this?

I brought my master news of Juliet's death and then very quickly he came from Mantua to this same place, to this same monument. This letter he asked me earlier to give to his father and threatened me with death, as he went into the vault, if I did not depart and leave him there.

Give me the letter; I will look at it. Where is the county [*Paris*] page, that summoned the watch? Sirrah, what was your master doing in this place?

He came with flowers to scatter his lady's grave and asked me to stand at a distance and so I did: soon, someone came with a light to open the tomb and by and by my master drew his sword on him and then I ran away to get the guards.

Prince

  This letter doth make good the friar's words,
Their course of love, the tidings of her death:
And here he writes that he did buy a poison
Of a poor 'pothecary, and therewithal
Came to this vault to die, and lie with Juliet.
Where be these enemies? Capulet! Montague!
See, what a scourge is laid upon your hate,
That heaven finds means to kill your joys with love.
And I for winking at your discords too
Have lost a brace of kinsmen: all are punish'd.

Capulet

  O brother Montague, give me thy hand:
This is my daughter's jointure, for no more
Can I demand.

Montague

  But I can give thee more:
For I will raise her statue in pure gold;
That while Verona by that name is known,
There shall no figure at such rate be set
As that of true and faithful Juliet.

Capulet

  As rich shall Romeo's by his lady's lie;
Poor sacrifices of our enmity!

Prince

  A glooming peace this morning with it brings;
The sun, for sorrow, will not show his head:
Go hence, to have more talk of these sad things;
Some shall be pardon'd and some punished:
For never was a story of more woe
Than this of Juliet & her Romeo.

       Exeunt

This letter does make good the friar's words, their course of love, the news of her death and here he writes that he did buy a poison off a poor apothecary and then finally he came to this vault to die and lie with Juliet. Where are these enemies? Capulet! Montague! See, what a suffering is laid upon your hate, that heaven finds means to kill your joys with love. And I for turning a blind eye to your conflict have also lost a pair of kinsmen (*Mercutio & Paris*): all are punished.

Oh brother Montague, give me your hand: this is my daughter's dowry, for no more can I give.

But I can give you more: for I will build a statue of her in pure gold that while Verona is still called Verona there shall be no statue as valuable as that of true and faithful Juliet.

As expensive a statue of Romeo will by his lady lie: poor sacrifices of our feud!

[*Some shall be...* : Steevens *suspected this was a reference to the original novel from whence Shakespeare wrote this play, where indeed the remaining characters are all subsequently judged for their accountability*]

103

Commentary : Act V

Apparently the Capulets lived in Mantua when Juliet was born [I.III]. As Balthasar arrives, for a moment, we always think everything is going to be okay. For first time viewers, we are expecting this to be the point when everything is explained to Romeo and we accelerate into a climax before the two lovers make it away together, happily ever after. For those of us who know better, there is still – especially when we perceive it performed on the stage – there is still this kind of fool's hope, this childish fancy that maybe, just maybe, this time, things work out differently. They never do.

The Apothecary is a kind of ghoulish spectre, someone physically half-way between life and death but also mentally half-way between life and death, between reality and the darker currents of the other side. Now we have a poison for her and a poison for him. We sense the return of the equilibrium at hand, only it jars in the place where Juliet is supposed to be dead. The Apothecary resists only a little, more as though he is checking it is not a set-up rather than any form of respect for the law and relinquishes his venomous cordial grudgingly to the desperate young man at his door.

As Romeo and Balthasar race back to Verona, the falling dominoes that have split their path begin to re-join their routes again and we quickly see Friar Laurence being given the heads-up that his plan is all going to hell. At the tomb, Paris, Romeo, Juliet, Friar Laurence and eventually everybody will end up having a good old cry. Once again, we are baffled at Romeo's sudden flashes of profound wisdom – he kills Paris, quite understandably, because Paris is so wrapped up in his own vain bereavement that Romeo is hardly capable of persuading him to let pass. But how admirably does Romeo treat the death of his enemy after he has slain him! He obliges Paris in his last wish, despite there being a clear conflict of interest and brings him inside the tomb. I always watch the actor carefully when Romeo can't remember whether Balthasar told him Paris was engaged to wed Juliet or not (*"Said he not so? Or did I it dream it so?"*) and I find it pleasing that Shakespeare not only follows his character's trail of thought so seamlessly during monologues and dialogue but that he even follows it outside of the narrative, concerning times and places that are never, in fact, depicted on stage. Shakespeare has truly captured Romeo's *state of mind*.

As Romeo gorges his eyes on Juliet's beauty one last time, to use the term 'dramatic irony' is entirely inadequate. Try 'perjury in the first degree' or 'murder through gross neglect'. *"Death, that hath suck'd the honey of thy breath, hath had no power yet upon thy beauty: Thou art not conquer'd; beauty's ensign yet is crimson in thy lips and in thy cheeks and death's pale flag is not advanced there,"* Romeo whispers in her ear, hovering over her, an invisible timer ticking all around him, the thoughts of the entire audience all screaming at him, like some kind of sick, mute pantomime.

Something the Elizabethans were obsessed with and is constantly explored in Shakespeare is the notion of dying in a 'state of grace'. Christian doctrine explains that the manner in which a person dies contributes a fantastic amount to their experience of the afterlife. If one dies at a ripe old age, asleep, with peace of mind and a content soul, or even if at some climatic moment of great importance they sacrifice themselves selflessly, then their entry into the next life is calm, illuminating and wholesome. You will float up on into heaven, even retaining some vague notions and fragments of memory from your life before, which will slowly fade like the gentle ebbing away of sands on a calm beach. If, on the other hand, you have a nightmare about drowning then awake only to die at the hands of two thugs holding your head into a barrel of wine, for instance, or if someone has their throat slit after being told they will be baked into a pie and unwittingly fed to their own parents, or if you are having an afternoon nap when your brother creeps in and pours a vile poison in your ear that courses through the veins of your blood, sending you into a convulsive seizure, boils breaking out all over your face and body, writhing in agony as the leperous distilment fizzes into your brain, then no matter the righteous and humble existence of your time in this world, your release from this 'mortal coil' is a painful, demonic, purgative experience. Do not collect 200 as you pass GO, instead go directly to the dark side of the lunar-sphere for a much needed and unimaginably painful stripping away of human desire, memories and earthly association. There is a fantastic scene in *Henry VI, Part 3* [I.IV] where Queen Margaret attempts to bait York into a twisted rage – and she succeeds quite fantastically as York spits insults at her that would put even Simon Cowell to shame – all in order to ensure that when York has his head lopped off a moment later he is feeling so bitter with hate, so tortured and in such mental agony that he goes directly to purgatory with no chance of a heavenly embrace. When Romeo commits suicide he does not do it in our modern contemporary sense - that once he dies his consciousness vanishes and he is relieved of his emotions - but rather he is only just then beginning to plunge into the depths of despair and suffering that we mortals cannot even contemplate. Romeo does not exactly commit suicide to escape a world without Juliet, as much as he is condemning his soul to aeons of misery where he can be alone with his grief and not have to endure the trivialities of every day life. Perhaps you are familiar with this feeling; ever had to let someone go? Ever smoked from dusk till dawn, in between staring with your eye-sockets at a television you can't see, through a constant watery glaze, channel surfing and forcing food into the vegetable called your body to sustain it just in case, one day, you feel like 'living' again? Well, that's how Romeo feels only much, much worse or you wouldn't be here to read this.

The most painful thing I hear Juliet say is *"Thy lips are warm,"* as she kisses Romeo's corpse. Seconds divide her from a happy ending, if only the Friar had arrived minutes earlier, and it kills me to see her realise that she was so close to awaking in her lover's arms. So close, but not close enough.

Returning to something I touched on in the introduction, *Romeo & Juliet* represent very real, specific times in our actual lives. Sooner or later there comes a time in everybody's life, a special twilight zone situated after we discover the burning, lustful feelings of sexual desire and before the reality of 'love being something we choose' sinks in; this magic hour is the event chronicled in abstract through *Romeo & Juliet*, at least it seems that way to me. Even the most hardened men of the world will sense something memorable about Juliet and every one of them will understand Romeo intimately. Women being much more in touch with our emotional intellect probably remember Romeo with quite some nostalgia and equally superior is their recognition of Juliet, which at some point or other was probably *exactly* what they were like, if ever they were like a lady.

Reading, watching, just *thinking* about *Romeo & Juliet* really takes us there, back to that special prime-time. It gives us access to 'hardship's sweet milk, philosophy' and lets us drink that calcium rich, bone building soul syrup that can become quite addictive. Looking back across the play, I suppose there is only one question worth asking: was it all worth it? Obviously, it is never a good idea for young people to commit suicide and it should be noted that neither of them would have, had Romeo known Juliet was still alive. So if we concede their deaths were a *mistake*, despite being self-inflicted, were the <u>two evenings and an afternoon at church</u> they spent together worth all those tears? This is the only question left behind after the play. What is the answer? Hell no? Of course it was? Let me pose the question in a different way; if we adopt my hypothesis about what the story represents, was that tragic heartache and devastation *you* endured worth the good times *you* spent with *your* first love? Do you look back now and regret it ever happening at all or do you thank life that you were lucky enough to experience that, even if only once? I cannot answer that question, I do not know you. But I tell you now, whatever the answer to that personal question is will be exactly the same as the answer to the play's.

Romeo, doff thy name,
And for thy name, which
is no part of thee,
Take all myself.